D1129856

The Queen
and the
Commonwealth

The Queen
and the
Commonwealth

TREVOR McDONALD

with Peter Tiffin

Thames Methuen

First published in Great Britain 1986
by Methuen London Ltd
11 New Fetter Lane, London EC4P 4EE
in association with
Thames Television International Ltd
149 Tottenham Court Road, London W1P 9LL
Copyright © 1986 Trevor McDonald, Peter Tiffin
Printed in Great Britain
by Hazell Watson & Viney Ltd
Member of the BPCC Group
Aylesbury, Bucks

British Library Cataloguing in Publication Data

McDonald, Trevor
  The Queen and the Commonwealth.
  1. Elizabeth II, *Queen of Great Britain*
  2. Great Britain – Kings and rulers – Biography
  3. Commonwealth of Nations – History
  I. Title
  II. Tiffin, Peter
  941.085′092′4   DA590

  ISBN 0–423–01900–7

Contents

List of Illustrations   vii
Acknowledgements   xi
Preface   xiii

1 What is the Commonwealth?   1
2 The Queen's first tour   20
3 India and Asia   40
4 Australasia   62
5 Africa   82
6 Canada   101
7 The West Indies   118
8 The Commonwealth Games   135
9 The Commonwealth in action   153
10 The future of the Commonwealth   173

Appendix A: The Queen's Commonwealth Tours   181
Appendix B: The Declaration of Commonwealth
         Principles   184
Index   187

Illustrations

page   *xvii* Her Majesty broadcasting to the Commonwealth, Christmas 1953

     3 The first Colonial Conference, 1887

     4 *above* The 1911 Imperial Conference

     4 *below* The 1926 Imperial Conference with King George V

     7 The 1948 Commonwealth meeting

     9 Her Majesty the Queen with Commonwealth heads of government, 1957

     12 Flags of the Commonwealth

     15 A state dinner at Buckingham Palace, 1977

     18 A 'family photo' taken on board *Britannia*, 1985

     22 Touring Jamaica, 1953

     23 Crossing the equator, 1953

     24 Fijian chiefs 'invite' the Queen to land, 1953

     25 A Tongan feast for the Queen, 1953

     26 An enthusiastic welcome to New Zealand in 1953

     27 The Queen's first Christmas away from home

     30 The Queen leaving Parliament House in Adelaide, Australia

     31 An Australian address of welcome to the Royal couple, 1954

     32 The Queen visits HMAS *Australia*

     33 A warm welcome in the Cocos Islands

     34 *above* Opening parliament in Ceylon, 1954

     34 *below* Walking in the heat to a rock fortress in Ceylon

     35 The Queen and Prince Philip visit ancient ruins in Ceylon

     36 The Queen with her children in Malta, 1954

     37 *Britannia* comes up the Thames on the way home, 1954

     42 The Queen driving through Delhi, 1961

     43 Her Majesty with Pandit Nehru, 1961

     44 *above* A visit to Gandhi's tomb, 1961

     44 *below* The Queen in a ceremonial barge on the Ganges, 1961

     45 Pausing among the lakes and gardens of the Taj Mahal, 1961

     46 An elephant ride for Her Majesty, 1961

     47 A stop on the way to the famous Khyber Pass, 1961

     48 A Valentine Day gift for the Queen from the children of Dhaka, 1961

     50 A glittering state banquet

     51 Local women display pottery to the Queen in a village just outside Delhi

     52 Coming face to face with poverty in the Commonwealth, Bangladesh, 1983

     53 The Queen with Mother Teresa of Calcutta, 1983

page 55 The Queen with Mrs Indira Gandhi, 1983
58 A visit to a rubber plantation in Malaysia, 1972
60 The state opening of Parliament in Mauritius, 1972
61 The Queen in Hong Kong, 1975
63 A spectacular arrival in Sydney, Australia, 1954
65 A surf carnival in Australia
66 A children's rally in Adelaide
71 Children greet the Queen in New Zealand, 1954
72 *above* An explanation about sheep-shearing in New Zealand
72 *below* The Queen opening parliament in Wellington, 1963
73 A sea of union flags greets the Queen in New Zealand
74 Her Majesty talking to Maoris
77 The Queen carried shoulder-high on her arrival in Cook Island, 1974
78 The Queen is carried in a decorated canoe on her 1982 visit to Tuvalu
79 *above left* The Royal couple with Queen Salote of Tonga, 1953
79 *above right* A roast pig is borne to the table for the Jubilee feast in Samoa, 1977
79 *below left* The Queen shares a joke with her Samoan host
79 *below right* The Queen with the King of Tonga
80 Receiving gifts from Cook Islanders
81 The Royal party on Pentecost Island, 1974
83 *above* The Queen is given a traditional Nigerian welcome, 1956
83 *below* The horsemen of Kaduna, Nigeria line the route to greet the Queen
84 Inspecting the Sword of Honour in Lagos
85 The Queen is shown a blacksmith's shop in Sierra Leone, 1961
86 *left and right* Gifts of flowers from children in Nigeria
87 The Ghanaian leader, Kwame Nkrumah, asks the Queen to dance, 1961
88 *above* Ghanaian tribesmen await the Queen's arrival, 1961
88 *below* Ghanaian women line the Queen's route
89 A sun hat for the Duke of Edinburgh in Ghana, 1961
93 Children dancing for the Queen in Botswana, 1979
96 *above* Dr Hastings Banda introduces Her Majesty to some of his countrywomen, 1979
96 *below* A tête-à-tête with Kenneth Kaunda in Lusaka, 1979
97 The Queen with Jomo Kenyatta, 1972
102 Opening Parliament in Ottawa, 1957
104 *above and below* The Queen never forgets Canada's indigenous peoples – the Indians and Eskimos
106 *above* Her Majesty wearing her famous 'Maple Leaf of Canada' dress, 1957
106 A Royal encounter at Whitehorse
108 The Queen in Charlottetown at a Gala Night presented in her honour
110 Cutting the cake at Canada's centenary celebrations, 1967
112 *above* The 1970 visit to the North-West Territories was a family affair

page 112 *below* On board *Britannia* going through the ever-present red boxes

113 A speech in Ottawa during the exhaustive 1977 Jubilee tour

116 *above* Prince Charles accompanying his mother to a Women's Institute bazaar

116 *below* The Queen inspects a traditional embroidered quilt

119 Crowds cheer the Queen on her visit to a straw market in Nassau, 1966

121 *above* A warm welcome from schoolchildren on St Kitts

121 *below* A local woman shows her affection for the Royal Family on the 1966 tour

124 *above* The Queen stops to chat to Antiguans on her 1985 tour

124 *below* The Queen knighting Gary Sobers, 1975

128 *above* Nassau decked out for the Queen's arrival, 1985

128 *below* The population of Nassau demonstrate dissatisfaction with their Prime Minister

132 *Britannia* under fireworks

133 The main conference room at Nassau, 1985

137 Australian Lorraine Crapp with members of the Ghana team in Cardiff, 1958

140 The British Empire and Commonwealth Games, 1958

141 Competitors at the 1958 Games

142 Prince Philip presenting medals at Cardiff

143 A boxing event at Cardiff

145 The 440-yards men's hurdle in Perth, 1962

147 *above* The legendary Kip Keino of Keyna leading the field, 1970

147 *below* The first ever 1500-metres race for women, 1970

150 Her Majesty at the award ceremony, Christchurch, 1974

151 *above and below* Colourful ceremonies at the Commonwealth Games in Brisbane, 1982

154 Marlborough House, the home of the Commonwealth Secretariat

155 Commonwealth Secretary-General Shridath Ramphal

158 *above* The Green Drawing-Room, where guests gather for receptions

158 *below* A Commonwealth Day reception at Marlborough House

164 The 1969 Commonwealth heads of government meeting

167 The Queen leaving Westminster Abbey after a Commonwealth Day service

171 The Queen at home with her Beefeaters in Britain

178 & 179 The young people of the Commonwealth

The authors and publisher would like to thank the following for their kind permission to reproduce illustrations: Topham Picture Library: xvii, 27, 36, 53, 63, 65, 71, 85, 142; the Royal Commonwealth Society: 3, 4 (above); 4 (below), 7; Press Association Photos: 9, 15; Photographers International: 18, 93, 96 (above), 104 (above), 121 (above), 124 (above); the Commonwealth Secretariat: 12–13, 155, 158 (below), 164; the Lord Chamberlain: 154, 158 (above); Popperfoto: 22, 23, 24, 30, 31, 33, 34 (above), 34 (below), 35, 37, 44 (above), 44 (below), 45, 47, 48, 66, 79 (above left), 83 (above), 83 (below), 86 (right), 87, 88 (above), 88 (below), 89, 102, 106 (above), 106 (below), 110, 119, 137, 143, 147 (above), 147 (below); Photo Source Ltd: 25, 32, 145; BBC Hulton Picture Library: 26, 72 (above), 81, 84, 86 (left), 113, 124 (below), 140, 141; Reginald Davis: 42, 43, 46, 50, 51, 61, 72 (below), 73, 74, 77, 80, 104 (below), 108, 112 (above), 116 (above), 150, 171; Syndication International: 52; Tim Graham: 55, 78, 79 (below left), 79 (below right), 167; John Scott: 58, 79 (above right), 96 (below), 116 (below), 178; Lord Lichfield: 60, 97, 112 (below); *Illustrated London News*: 121 (below), 132; Anna Arki: 128 (above); Peter Tiffin: 128 (below), 133, 179; All-Sport Photographic Ltd: 151 (above), 151 (below).

The map on pages xiv–xv was drawn by Neil Hyslop from information supplied by the Commonwealth Secretariat.

Acknowledgements

This book originated in the Thames television programme 'The Queen and the Commonwealth', made to mark the Queen's sixtieth birthday. It was written and narrated by Trevor McDonald and produced and directed by Peter Tiffin for the Documentary Department of Thames Television. It is therefore appropriate that our first duty is to thank Catherine Freeman, the Controller of Documentaries and Features at Thames Television for giving us the opportunity to make the film.

The single most important fact about this endeavour, film and book, has been the willingness and enthusiasm of people to talk about the role of the Queen in relation to the modern Commonwealth. At the Commonwealth heads of government meeting in Nassau in the Bahamas in October 1985, they all gave freely of their time and were positively delighted to talk about the significant influence of the Queen on the Commonwealth. We are also grateful to former British prime ministers, senior politicians and Commonwealth and constitutional experts who agreed to see us in this country.

Nearer home our greatest debt is to our tireless researcher, Anna Arki, who not only guided us with a deft hand through the great body of existing work on the Commonwealth, but who must now hold the record for setting up interviews with the greatest number of prime ministers at any one conference. She was also responsible for the painstaking work that went into the picture research. In our travels in the Caribbean and Africa, as production assistant, Jill Baldrey mastered the logistics with cheerful skill. We would also like to thank all the Thames Television film crews and electricians who worked on the film, in particular cameraman Peter

George, his assistant Chris Ward and sound recordist Ron Thomas, who were with us throughout, and our cheerful and patient film editor Maggie Knox.

It is difficult to imagine that there is any journalist or writer who knows more about Commonwealth affairs than Derek Ingram of Gemini News Service. His advice and encouragement were life-sustaining. And we would like to thank André Deutsch Ltd for granting us permission to reproduce extracts from *Stitches in Time* by Arnold Smith with Clyde Sanger, published in 1981; and Macmillan London Ltd for granting us permission to reproduce extracts from *The Evolution of the Modern Commonwealth, 1902–80* by Dennis Judd and Peter Slinn, published in 1982.

One can never hope to find an organization more helpful than the Commonwealth Secretariat at Marlborough House. All the Secretariat's officials were happy to give freely of their time, and the indefatigable Patsy Robertson was a tower of strength. Her suggestions were unfailingly useful.

A personal debt of gratitude is owed to the Editor of ITN's Channel Four News, Stewart Purvis, and to ITN's Editor, David Nicholas, for giving Trevor the time to do the Thames Television programme and to complete this book. Theirs was an act of great kindness.

And it was comforting to have Rebekah Ponsford and Jill Baldrey to tidy up and type the manuscript, after it had received the much-appreciated attentions of our editor at Thames Methuen, Alex Bennion.

Preface

This book is not concerned solely with the Commonwealth or with the many and varied multi-national assistance projects in which the Commonwealth is involved. Nor is it meant to be a definitive book about Her Majesty the Queen. It is rather a celebration of the Queen's role as Head of the Commonwealth and of Her Majesty's devotion to the Commonwealth ideal.

That devotion is reflected in almost everything the Queen says about the Commonwealth, and in her busy schedule of international travel in which visits to Commonwealth countries are given a pre-eminent place.

The Queen's declared personal faith in the Commonwealth and her dedication to what it stands for have helped to make the organisation the forward-looking contemporary international instrument it has become. No other international body can claim a leader so dedicated to its cause, so proud of its origins and its diversity, so convinced of its usefulness as a positive force for good in the world. And her faith and devotion are amply repaid by Commonwealth heads of government, who regard the Queen as the crucial symbol of their unity in a world torn apart by strife and dissent.

From the South Seas to northern Canada, from the depths of Central Africa to the Indian sub-continent and the Antipodes, from South-East Asia to the Caribbean, the Queen's standing in the Commonwealth remains an enviable phenomenon in the modern world. And the fact that this body continues to flourish and to grow is due in no small part to the personality, wisdom and determination of Her Majesty.

The voices of her people – high and low, across barriers of race, colour and religion – sing out the value of what she herself calls 'the Commonwealth family, this remarkable collection of friendly people'.

One tribal chief in Papua New Guinea said of her: 'She is not only wonderful, but she is a woman too.' In India, on a state drive, as the crowds shouted 'Long Live the Queen', one man was heard to exclaim: 'She's the most wonderful Queen in the world.' When the Queen went to Zambia in 1979, acting on her own initiative and despite concern for her personal safety, a Zambian priest likened her arrival to the Second Coming and one newspaper proclaimed boldly that 'she could be Queen of all the world'.

That is the esteem in which Her Majesty is held. That is how the respectful Commonwealth sees its Head.

	Country	Population+	Capital	Govern- ment	Date of Joining			Country	Population+	Capital	Govern- ment	Date of Joining
1	Antigua & Barbuda	100,000	St Johns	M	1981		16	Lesotho	1,400,000	Maseru	M*	1966
2	Bahamas	200,000	Nassau	M	1973		17	Malawi	6,200,000	Lilongwe	R	1964
3	Barbados	300,000	Bridgetown	M	1966		18	Malta	400,000	Valletta	R	1964
4	Belize	100,000	Belmopan	M	1981		19	Nigeria	87,600,000	Lagos	R	1960
5	Botswana	900,000	Gaborone	R	1966		20	St Christopher-Nevis	50,000	Basseterre	M	1983
6	Britain	56,000,000	London	M			21	St Lucia	100,000	Castries	M	1979
7	Canada	24,200,000	Ottawa	M	1931§		22	St Vincent & Grenadines	100,000	Kingstown	M	1979
8	Cyprus	600,000	Nicosia	R	1961		23	Sierra Leone	3,600,000	Freetown	R	1961
9	Dominica	100,000	Roseau	R	1978		24	Swaziland	600,000	Mbabane	M*	1968
10	The Gambia	600,000	Banjul	R	1965		25	Tanzania	19,100,000	Dar es Salaam	R	1961
11	Ghana	11,800,000	Accra	R	1957		26	Trinidad & Tobago	1,200,000	Port of Spain	R	1962
12	Grenada	100,000	St George's	M	1974		27	Uganda	13,000,000	Kampala	R	1962
13	Guyana	800,000	Georgetown	R	1966		28	Zambia	5,800,000	Lusaka	R	1964
14	Jamaica	2,200,000	Kingston	M	1962		29	Zimbabwe	7,200,000	Harare	R	1980
15	Kenya	17,400,000	Nairobi	R	1963							

Countries of the Commonwealth

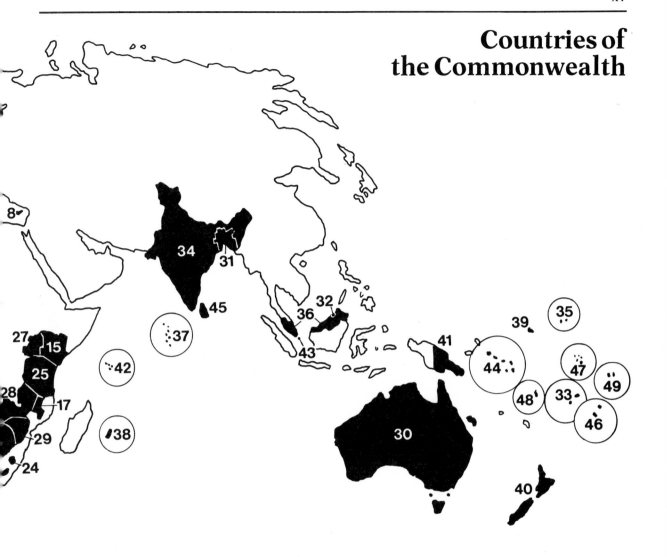

	Country	Population+	Capital	Govern-ment	Date of Joining
30	Australia	14,900,000	Canberra	M	1931§
31	Bangladesh	90,700,000	Dhaka	R	1972
32	Brunei	220,000	Bandar Seri Begawan	M*	1984
33	Fiji	600,000	Suva	M	1970
34	India	733,200,000	New Delhi	R	1947
35	Kiribati	60,000	Tarawa	R	1979
36	Malaysia	14,200,000	Kuala Lumpur	M*	1957
37	Maldives	200,000	Malé	R	1982
38	Mauritius	900,000	Port Louis	M	1968
39	Nauru	8,000	Nauru	R	1968
40	New Zealand	3,300,000	Wellington	M	1931§
41	Papua New Guinea	3,100,000	Port Moresby	M	1975
42	Seychelles	100,000	Victoria	R	1976
43	Singapore	2,400,000	Singapore	R	1965
44	Solomon Islands	200,000	Honiara	M	1978

	Country	Population+	Capital	Govern-ment	Date of Joining
45	Sri Lanka	15,000,000	Columbo	R	1948
46	Tonga	100,000	Nuku'alofa	M*	1970
47	Tuvalu	8,000	Funafuti	M	1978
48	Vanuatu	100,000	Port Vila	R	1980
49	Western Samoa	200,000	Apia	R	1970

Nauru and Tuvalu are special members. They participate in functional meetings and activities, but do not attend meetings of Heads of Government.

M	Monarchy with Queen Elizabeth, who is represented by a Governor-General in all countries except Britain
M*	National Monarchy
R	Republic
+	Figures from the World Bank Atlas
1931§	Statute of Westminster

The Queen and the Commonwealth

'We belong, you and I, to a far larger family.
We belong, all of us to the . . . Commonwealth,
that immense union of nations, with their homes
set in all the four corners of the earth.'
HER MAJESTY THE QUEEN

'Her Majesty reinforces by her very presence
the family aspect of the Commonwealth.'
BRIAN MULRONEY *Canadian Prime Minister*

'She's a great person; she's a leader among leaders.'
KENNETH KAUNDA *Zambian President*

'I think she's got . . . the most difficult job in the
world and I think she discharges it with . . .
composure, commitment and dedication.'
ROBERT HAWKE *Australian Prime Minister*

'When I talk to her about my country,
I feel she knows what I'm talking about.'
DR MAHATHIR MOHAMED *Malaysian Prime Minister*

'Well! Why should I be impressed? I should have known
she has a complete grasp of everything that's happening.'
EUGENIA CHARLES *Dominican Prime Minister*

'Without Her Majesty's role as Head of the Commonwealth
the association wouldn't have that unity.'
MARGARET THATCHER *British Prime Minister*

'The one person who symbolises the continuing health
of that transformation from Empire to Commonwealth
is Her Majesty the Queen.'
RAJIV GANDHI *Indian Prime Minister*

'She holds the Commonwealth together.
She is the key figure.'
DAVID LANGE *New Zealand Prime Minister*

'The Commonwealth . . . is an entirely new conception. . . .
To that new conception of an equal partnership
of nations and races I shall give myself,
heart and soul, every day of my life.'
HER MAJESTY THE QUEEN

*Her Majesty
broadcasting to the
Commonwealth,
Christmas 1953*

CHAPTER 1

What is the Commonwealth?

'The Commonwealth bears no resemblance to the Empires
of the past. It is an entirely new conception . . . built on the
highest qualities of the spirit of man: friendship, loyalty
and the desire for freedom and peace.'
HER MAJESTY THE QUEEN Christmas Broadcast, 1953

'Its justification lies in its very existence.'
JULIUS NYERERE *Former Tanzanian President*

Referring to the fact that the modern Commonwealth
grew out of the old British Empire, the Prime Minister of
Singapore, Lee Kuan Yew, is fond of saying: 'We were, all
of us, once citizens of Rome.' Her Majesty would
appreciate the metaphor, but she has always insisted
that the Commonwealth 'bears no resemblance to the
Empires of the past'. And few Commonwealth leaders
would disagree. On the contrary, they would explain
their attachment to the association and the fact that it
has survived the most turbulent period of our modern
history – defusing along the way some of the most
potentially damaging political issues of our time – by
making the point that the Commonwealth is different
from any other political or economic grouping in the
world.

The modern Commonwealth is a union of equal
partners but, as Lee Kuan Yew suggests, it cannot be
seen in its proper perspective unless we understand its
origins.

At the dawn of the twentieth century there was not a
climate or continent in which the British flag did not fly,
though the Empire began to decline as soon as it reached

its apogee. In the words of Dennis Judd and Peter Slinn, authors of *The Evolution of the Modern Commonwealth*, the British stamped

> a clear, although sometimes light, mark on a vast conglomeration of territories and people. Britain provided the administrative personnel and much of the investment, just as she dominated the Empire's trade. The British monarch, the English language, English legal and constitutional procedures, even educational standards, helped to link the component parts of the Empire together.

At its height, 13 million square miles of the world's map was covered in the familiar red of the British Empire, and 360 million of the world's population owed allegiance to the British Crown. This allegiance to the Crown was common to all; but in many other respects Britain's relationship with the countries of its Empire varied considerably.

Firstly there were the original countries of white settlement: Canada, Australia, New Zealand and South Africa. These were the dominions, a term which implied a substantial amount of self-government.

Then there was the vast sub-continent that we know as India, stretching from Kashmir and the Himalayas in the north to the island of Ceylon in the south. It had been an empire in its own right since 1876. There was a Secretary of State for India in the British Cabinet, but it was the Viceroy in Delhi who governed with the help of the massive Indian Civil Service, staffed mainly by Indians.

Across the rest of the world were the Crown colonies, acquired by Britain at different times and almost invariably because of the trade or strategic advantage that would accrue to Britain. On islands in the Caribbean and the South Pacific, in the treacherous climate of the Gambia and the Gold Coast of West Africa to the steaming jungles and rubber plantations of Malaya and Burma, the British Colonial Service took responsibility for government.

Lastly, there were the Middle East protectorates.

Although Egypt and Sudan had been under British rule since the 1880s, Palestine, Jordan and Iraq all became the responsibility of the British either during or after the First World War as the old Turkish–Ottoman Empire disintegrated. Whatever reputation Britain may have gained as sympathetic and progressive in its treatment of countries making their way to independence, this did not apply in the Middle East, where Britain's presence was short, sharp and painful. When their independence was achieved in the 1950s and 60s none of these countries chose to join the Commonwealth.

On the occasion of Queen Victoria's Golden Jubilee in 1887, representatives of the colonial governments were summoned to a Colonial Conference in London. Colonial Conferences, later to be known as Imperial Conferences, were held regularly to discuss the problems of Britain's far-flung responsibilities. And it was at the Imperial Conference of 1926, under the chairmanship of Lord Balfour – a former Conservative Prime Minister – that

The first Colonial Conference was held in London in 1887 and was attended by representatives from Canada, Newfoundland, New Zealand, the Cape of Good Hope, Natal and Australia

*The 1911 Imperial
Conference set up a
Royal Commission
on the dominions*

*1926. The first
photograph to show
the monarch, King
George V, with con-
ference participants
from Britain,
Canada, Australia,
New Zealand, South
Africa, Newfound-
land and the Irish
Free State*

the first attempt was made to define the constitutional relationship that existed between Britain and its self-governing dominions.

The Balfour formula of 1926, which five years later was to become law as the Statute of Westminster, stated that: 'dominions . . . are autonomous communities within the British Empire, equal in status, in no way subordinate to one another . . . though united by common allegiance to the Crown'.

This was an entirely new concept of Commonwealth, but some twenty years later, when India – in one of the greatest peaceful revolutions of all time – became independent, this definition had to be significantly altered. To the Indian Congress Party it seemed that the 1926 definition of the Commonwealth was merely a clever device to give some political autonomy to the countries concerned, but to keep real political control in British hands. One Viceroy put it honestly in 1945 when he said that if Britain were to secure India 'as a friendly partner in the British Commonwealth, our predominant influence in these countries will . . . be assured; with a lost and hostile India, we are likely to be reduced in the East to the position of commercial bagmen'.

Sir Stafford Cripps agreed. 'My great anxiety,' he wrote to Churchill, 'is to keep India within the Commonwealth of our nations because I believe that it is of very great importance to our future position in the world both economically and politically.'

The man chosen by the Attlee Government to preside over the granting of Indian independence was the King's cousin, Louis Mountbatten, and he was given the specific task of ensuring that India remained within the Commonwealth. This instruction had come from the King himself.

India was offered dominion status, but Nehru saw this as a clumsy attempt to compromise Indian independence. So with consummate tactical brilliance he spearheaded the support for a resolution in Congress that India was to become a sovereign republic. That, Nehru reasoned, would keep the link with the Crown at an appropriate distance.

Mountbatten, without consulting Whitehall, said he saw nothing irreconcilable between India's desire to make its independence real and Britain's wish that it should remain as a member of the Commonwealth. The device that was used was remarkably simple. The fundamental objection of the Indian Congress party was to the untenability of a republic owing allegiance to the Crown, however free and independent it might be in all other respects. But there was no such objection to the King being a 'symbol' of the association. In fact, quite the opposite.

In the words of Sir David Hunt, then a senior civil servant in the Dominions Office:

> We agreed to the King being Head of the Commonwealth, on the condition that he exercised no powers whatsoever, but that he was a token. Now this pleased all of them because it meant that there was really no shadow whatever on the independence and, secondly, because they were very attached to the Royal Family. . . . In Pakistan the King Emperor was a great favourite, and in Ceylon, of course, they remained a monarchy till very recently.

And so at the Commonwealth Prime Ministers' meeting in London in 1949 a declaration was issued which said: 'The Government of India declared and affirmed India's desire to continue her full membership of the Commonwealth of Nations, and her acceptance of the King as the symbol of the free association of its independent member nations and as such the *Head of the Commonwealth* [our italics].'

In one brilliantly innovative moment, therefore, the idea of the modern Commonwealth had been born. A blueprint had been arrived at to keep republics within the Commonwealth, and this was to ensure that nations of an immense variety of creeds, colours and cultures could make up what has become the modern Commonwealth.

Nehru made his historic 'tryst with destiny' speech in August 1947. He talked about his country stepping from

The first Commonwealth meeting attended by representatives of the newly independent states of India, Pakistan and Ceylon, 1948

'the old to the new, when an age ends and when the soul of a nation long suppressed finds utterance'. But by agreeing to stay in the Commonwealth club, he was striking a powerful blow for the start of its transformation. Until that time, the Commonwealth had been built around a small club of white nations but, by agreeing to join, India ensured the future development of the Commonwealth as an association of free states of all races and peoples. Their common characteristic was that they had all once been ruled by Britain. But the old club changed with its new membership to become a forward-looking body of professional people and brilliant politicians.

The United States of America had had reason to hope that Indian independence would end the dominance of British influence in that part of the world. But when India decided to stay within what the Queen today calls 'that immense union of nations, with their homes in all four corners of the earth' it took an American commentator, Walter Lippman, to see what a great triumph the birth of the new Commonwealth had been. He wrote:

> Perhaps Britain's finest hour is not yet in the past. Certainly this performance is not the work of a decadent people. This, on the contrary, is the work of political genius requiring the ripest wisdom and the freshest vigour and it's done with an elegance and a style that will compel and will receive an instinctive respect throughout the civilised world.

Years later, in a memorable phrase, Nehru said that in troubled times the Commonwealth provided a 'healing touch'.

Following the independence of India the Commonwealth leaders met sporadically in London. Their numbers had grown from five to eight to include the leaders of India, Pakistan and Ceylon. It was still a very small and élite group.

Then, in 1957, the first African colony became independent. Overnight the Gold Coast disappeared and the Republic of Ghana was born under the Presidency of Kwame Nkrumah. Over the following decades the British flag was gradually lowered as dozens of new independent states came into being across the world.

The end of Empire came peacefully for some, but for others there was pain and violence and prison for its leaders. Dr Hastings Banda, Life President of Malawi (once Nyasaland), was gaoled by the British. So too was Kenneth Kaunda, for twenty-two years the President of Zambia, who says:

> There is no doubt at all in my mind that if we did not have to struggle that long for independence, if we did not have to go to prison . . . I don't know whether we would have managed to go through the difficulties we've been going through. That was really good university education in preparation for our independence.

Both men are now among the Commonwealth's strongest advocates.

In Kenya there was armed conflict between the British and the Kikuyu terrorists known as Mau Mau. Jomo Kenyatta, later to become the country's first president, spent eight years in a British gaol. And the memory is still fresh of the fifteen-year struggle that finally brought Southern Rhodesia to Zimbabwe in 1980.

Over the rest of the world, there was war in Malaya between British armed forces and a communist guerilla army. It lasted for several years until the country became independent in 1957. And in Cyprus between 1948 and 1956 British forces were again in action against terror-

Her Majesty the Queen with Commonwealth heads of government in 1957, including Kwame Nkrumah from the first African state to achieve independence

ists who wanted the island to be united with Greece. Cyprus finally became independent in 1959 and Archbishop Makarios, released from exile in the Seychelles, later became its first President.

When independence eventually came to these countries, however hard and bitter had been the road to its attainment, it was marked by two remarkable features. Firstly, the independence celebrations were attended by a member of the British Royal Family and, secondly, almost all the newly independent states applied to join the Commonwealth. The Queen herself did not attend the ceremony marking the end of the rule of the British Crown in each country, but she did visit them at the earliest opportunity in her new role as Head of the Commonwealth.

Application to join the Commonwealth is open to all. It has never been refused and only a few have declined the opportunity. Among those countries which did not join is Burma, which became an independent republic in 1948, before the concept of a Head of Commonwealth had been devised. The Republic of Ireland had dominion status until the Anglo-Irish Treaty of 1921 formed the Irish Free State. But, as Judd and Slinn put it:

> This Agreement ensured that, generally, the position of the Free State in relation to the imperial parliament and the government should be that of the Dominion of Canada. Southern Ireland, however, could not take her place cosily as one of the daughters of the Commonwealth. Ireland was herself a mother country and not a colony of settlement, the source of the large 'Irish' communities in North America and Australia.
>
> Her leaders did not acknowledge any debt of gratitude to Britain for the concession of Irish 'freedom', no 'miracle of trust and magnanimity' such as had reconciled Boer leaders in South Africa. The Irish considered that they had won their freedom by force of arms, as was recognised implicitly by the negotiation of the Treaty in 1921. To them the imperial system was the hated

instrument of oppresion, so long the denial of
their national freedom. There were no Commonwealth men in the Southern Irish leadership,
sentimentally attached to the Crown and other
imperial symbols.

When Eamonn de Valera became Prime Minister in
1932 he devoted himself to severing the last formal links
between Southern Ireland and the Commonwealth. A
new constitution was adopted in 1937 which made
Ireland a republic in all but name and, although links
with the Commonwealth were not ended formally until
1949, Irish neutrality in 1939 meant the 'severing of all
intimate Commonwealth communications and relations
between the governments'.

Pakistan left the Commonwealth in 1971 after the
formation of Bangladesh, but the most notorious departure from the Commonwealth came with the withdrawal
of South Africa in 1961. There was universal opposition
to the country's apartheid policies, but the Commonwealth heads of government meeting held in London
that year started out with a determination to give South
Africa another chance. However, the truculent attitude
of the South African Prime Minister, Dr Verwoerd,
exasperated everyone and in the end he withdrew from
the meeting. Thus South Africa effectively expelled
itself from the Commonwealth.

Today the Commonwealth consists of forty-nine independent members embracing a vast range of the
world's peoples, of countless races, colours, cultures and
religious persuasions. Commonwealth countries range
in size from Tuvalu in the Pacific, with a population of
about 8000, to the vast sub-continent of India with its
population of 750 million. Some old dominions have
only one language, English, and are mirrors of English
life abroad. Others, like Brunei and Vanuatu, seem as
distant from any concept of Englishness as it is possible
to imagine.

The Commonwealth also embraces and finds a place
for a wide variety of governmental systems. These range

Flags of the Commonwealth

Antigua and Barbuda

Barbados

Brunei

Canada

The Gambia

Ghana

Grenada

Kenya

Kiribati

Lesotho

Malta

Mauritius

Nauru

St. Christopher and Nevis

Saint Lucia

St Vincent and the Grenadin

Solomon Islands

Sri Lanka

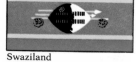
Swaziland

Tuvalu

Uganda

Vanuatu

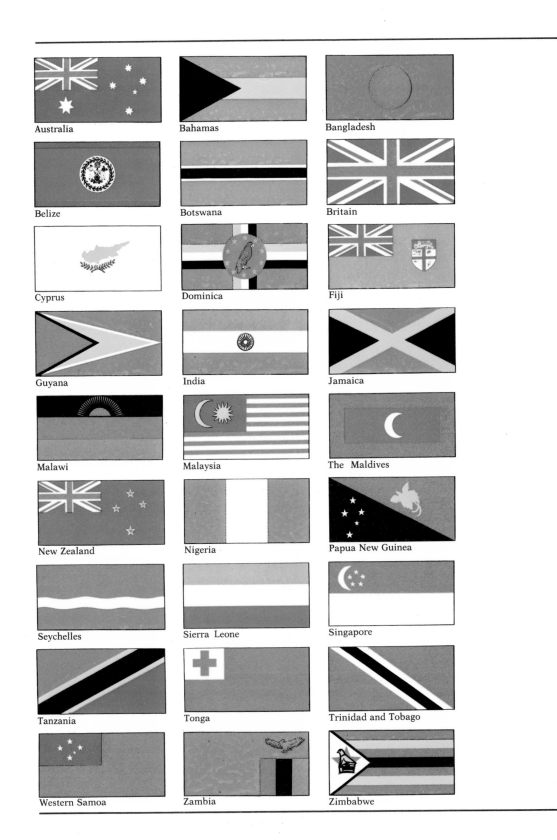

Australia	Bahamas	Bangladesh
Belize	Botswana	Britain
Cyprus	Dominica	Fiji
Guyana	India	Jamaica
Malawi	Malaysia	The Maldives
New Zealand	Nigeria	Papua New Guinea
Seychelles	Sierra Leone	Singapore
Tanzania	Tonga	Trinidad and Tobago
Western Samoa	Zambia	Zimbabwe

from Westminster-style democracies to one-party states, some of which verge on the dictatorial. But they all have one thing in common. All members of the Commonwealth accept the Queen as the symbol of their free association and accordingly as the Head of the Commonwealth. Most of the forty-nine members are republics with their own heads of state. But for seventeen countries, apart from the United Kingdom, the Queen is also head of state. She is the Queen of:

Antigua and Barbuda
Australia
Bahamas
Barbados
Belize
Canada
Fiji
Grenada
Jamaica
Mauritius
New Zealand
Papua New Guinea
St Christopher and Nevis
St Lucia
St Vincent and the Grenadines
Solomon Islands
Tuvalu

When the Queen visits these countries she performs the same duties as she does in Britain. In Grenada in 1985 she read the Speech from the Throne to the tiny Parliament in St George's, and a few weeks later at Westminster her Speech from the Throne outlined the government's legislative programme for the year.

The Queen's presence in a country in which she is head of state is obviously an exceptional circumstance. For the rest of the time the Queen's representative is the Governor-General. At one time he would have been sent out from London, but today the Governor-General will be a native of the country and will be appointed by the Queen on the advice of the Prime Minister of the country concerned. Although the Governor-General is the personal representative of the Queen, he does not seek instructions from her. He will act on his own authority, only informing her afterwards of what he has done. This has happened recently on two notable occasions. In Australia in November 1975 the Governor-General, Sir John Kerr, sacked Prime Minister Gough Whitlam; and in 1982 Sir Paul Scoon, Governor-General of Grenada, called in American forces to help his troubled island.

In addition to the eighteen countries of which the Queen is head of state, and the twenty-six republics, there are five Commonwealth countries – Malaysia, Lesotho, Swaziland, Tonga, and Brunei – which have their own indigenous monarchs.

This multi-national, multi-racial association is held together and nourished by the deep interest of Her Majesty the Queen. It is one thing that sets the

Commonwealth heads of government at a state dinner held at Buckingham Palace in the Queen's Jubilee year, 1977

Commonwealth apart from any other world body. The Queen takes her Commonwealth responsibilities extremely seriously, and is repaid in full by the respect of the Commonwealth heads of government.

The Canadian Prime Minister, Brian Mulroney, says: 'Her Majesty reinforces by her very presence the family aspect of the Commonwealth. And she is the prime force keeping the family together.' And Indian Prime Minister Rajiv Gandhi agrees: 'That is the major role played by Her Majesty the Queen. She represents the great unity. She holds the Commonwealth together. She is the key figure. We all look to her because of the great strength her presence and her influence give to the Commonwealth. That's the role played by the Queen. It's a major role and Her Majesty does it very well.'

The Prime Minister of Malaysia, Dr Mahathir Mohamed, says his country regards the Queen as a vital symbol:

> The Queen is the symbol of the origins and the unity of the Commonwealth. In any kind of grouping like this, you need to have a leader and the Queen could be regarded as the Commonwealth leader, without the executive authority, of course. But she provides the focus. She is the one who draws the whole thing together.

And all this is well summed up by the Prime Minister of New Zealand, David Lange:

> The Queen is the bit of glue that somehow manages to hold the whole thing together. She has a quiet but fairly pervasive presence at social functions. She is intelligent and acute when she speaks with Commonwealth leaders, to my judgement, and yet when it comes to a functional role, it is not there. She is very careful not to exercise that functional role which would be destructive of the bond, and I suppose it is to some extent a matter of worry that clearly her personality is a major factor to all of us in the Commonwealth. She does the unifying.

To promote that unity in the Commonwealth, the Queen sees Commonwealth prime ministers in London, keeps well up to date on Commonwealth affairs through the Foreign Office despatches, and travels extensively to Commonwealth countries around the world. As Prince Philip once said, these visits are not undertaken for the health of the Royal Family, and the Queen herself explained the 'one idea' which dominates her thinking on royal tours of the Commonwealth – 'the wish to foster and advance understanding within the Commonwealth. No purpose comes nearer to my desires.'

The Queen visits Commonwealth countries at the invitation of the head of government in those countries. And she receives invitations from countries where she is head of state and from republics alike. The Prime Minister of Dominica, Miss Eugenia Charles, says: 'We of course decided to become a republic. But when I saw her, I told the Queen that we would be very honoured to have a visit from her to Dominica. It would make our year.'

The Commonwealth has no common policy; the most burning issues which affect it are usually perceived as deriving from the wish of one Commonwealth member to put its own interests first while ignoring the interests of others. It has no rules or traditions. It has no real constitution to speak of, and no obvious power to affect the course of world affairs. It has no charter. The absence of either enables the conduct of its affairs to take place in an informal manner. Its meetings of heads of government do discuss international political affairs, but no formal resolutions or motions are passed. The Commonwealth tends to lean more towards statements of principle. It attempts to avoid damaging splits in its discussions and tries to achieve consensus, wherever possible.

Today, the Queen speaks of this flexible Commonwealth with perspicacity and realism:

We talk of ourselves as a 'family of nations' and perhaps our relations with one another are not so very different from those which exist between

members of any family. We know that these are
not always easy, for there is no law within a
family which binds its members to think, or act,
or be alike.

And surely it is this very freedom of choice and
decision which gives exceptional value to
friendship in times of stress and disagreement.
Such friendship is a gift for which we are truly
and rightly grateful.

*A 'family photo'
taken on board*
Britannia *during
the heads of govern-
ment meeting in
Nassau, 1985*

The modern Commonwealth survives partly because
its existence is nourished by the profound interest of the
Queen. Thus the association lasts despite the fact that it's
made up of governments of vastly different political
complexions. It continues to function despite the fact
that its members frequently disagree among themselves
about the major issues of international politics, and
although some members test the tolerance of others to
the limit.

Transcending all these differences is the essential
unifying force provided by the Queen. No one under-
stands that role better than Her Majesty herself. As long
ago as 1956 she said:

I believe that the way in which our Commonwealth is developing represents one of the most
imaginative experiments in international affairs
that the world has ever seen. If, as its Head, I can
make any real personal contribution towards its
progress, it must surely be to promote its unity.
... Deep and acute differences involving both
intellect and emotion are bound to arise between
members of a family and also between friend and
friend. In all such differences ... for the sake of
ultimate harmony, the healing power of tolerance, comradeship and love must be allowed to
play its part.

Today, there can be no better definition of the way in
which the modern Commonwealth functions, and of how
the Queen sees her role.

CHAPTER 2

The Queen's first tour

'The structure and framework of monarchy could easily
stand as an archaic and meaningless survival. We have
received visible and audible proof that it is living in the
hearts of the people.'
HER MAJESTY THE QUEEN, 1954

If there is one over-riding reason why there is such
universal affection and admiration for the Queen around
the Commonwealth it is that she has visited every single
one of the forty-nine states at some time during her reign.
The Royal tours have been a notable feature of her
thirty-three years on the throne. No previous monarch
has (nor, it must be said, could have) travelled so far and
so often.

The Queen's commitment to the Commonwealth came
early. On a coming-of-age tour of South Africa she
dedicated her life 'be it long or short . . . to your service
and the service of our great Imperial Commonwealth to
which we all belong.' This tour, with her parents and
sister, to the warmth and sunshine of South Africa
during Britain's bitter winter of 1947 had been a happy
one, although no doubt the young Princess would have
enjoyed it even more had one other name been included
in the guest-list. It was an open secret that the Princess
had already accepted Prince Philip's proposal of marriage, but the King insisted that any formal announcement of the engagement must wait until after the South
African tour.

The official announcement came in July 1947, the
marriage took place in November, and twelve months
later their first child was born, a son, followed two years
later by a daughter. But for her the life of a young mother,

whose principal dedication was to the bringing-up of her children, was not to last.

On 31 January 1952, King George VI saw Princess Elizabeth and Prince Philip leave London airport for an extended tour that was to include East Africa, Australia and New Zealand. But within a week of their departure the King had died in his sleep at Sandringham, and his daughter – 4000 miles away at a hunting-lodge, Treetops, in a Kenyan game reserve – succeeded to the throne at the age of twenty-five.

In her first ever Christmas Broadcast in 1952, the Queen stressed the importance of the Commonwealth as she saw it and her dedication to its ideals. Referring to the fact that at Christmas our thoughts 'are always full of homes and families', the Queen said:

> But we belong, you and I, to a far larger family. We belong, all of us, to the British Common-wealth and Empire, that immense union of nations, with their homes in all four corners of the earth. Like our own families, it can be a great power for good – a force which I believe can be of immeasurable benefit to all humanity. My father and grandfather before him worked all their lives to unite our peoples ever more closely, and to maintain its ideals which were so near to their hearts. I shall strive to carry on their work.

The commitment to Commonwealth that the young Princess Elizabeth had made on her twenty-first birth-day in South Africa, and then again in her first Christmas broadcast, was made real by the new Queen within months of her Coronation. She was crowned in Westminster Abbey in June 1953, and within five months she embarked on the most ambitious tour ever undertaken by any monarch. On a cold November evening the Queen and Prince Philip boarded the strato-cruiser *Canopus*, which was to take them on the first stage of an epic journey that would circumnavigate the globe.

Bermuda, the tiny holiday island in the Atlantic, was the first brief stop-over for the Royal couple. They stayed only a few hours before going on to the Caribbean island of Jamaica, where they were greeted with great enthusiasm and stayed for several days. After Jamaica, the pace of the first few days slowed down as the Royal couple boarded the SS *Gothic* for a leisurely three-week cruise across the Pacific Ocean to the romantic islands of Fiji and Tonga.

The beginning of a happy relationship with the Caribbean, Jamaica 1953

This was in the days before the *Britannia*, and on the way to Fiji Prince Philip took part with gusto in the ceremony known as 'crossing the line' whenever the Royal yacht sailed over the equator. According to one contemporary account of life on board the Royal yacht, engines stop at about sunset the day before the ship is due to cross the equator. From behind a screen rigged up on deck, King Neptune's messengers emerge to deliver an address of welcome to the ship, now 'entering Neptune's domains'. At the same time, they summon all those who have never crossed before to appear before Neptune's court at a certain time on the following day. The novices are given seats where they are lathered and shaved by the ship's barber and given a pill by the doctor. While this is in progress the seats are tipped up without warning and the poor novices are thrown helplessly into the ship's pool. For good measure, they are repeatedly ducked in the water.

The time-honoured 'ceremony' of ducking victims crossing the equator for the first time. Only Her Majesty was immune

Prince Philip, his nose red with greasepaint and a blue and white butcher's apron flapping round his legs, had a great time heaving luckless novices into the pool. The Queen filmed it all and was only saved from an undignified ducking herself on the grounds that she had undergone the ordeal once before during the cruise to South Africa seven years before.

On 17 December, when the SS *Gothic* sailed into Fijian waters, the Queen and Prince Philip were given a ritual welcome. Native chiefs went aboard to greet Her Majesty and present her with a necklace of whale's teeth. It was intended to signify a formal invitation to the Royal visitors to come ashore.

Fijian chiefs 'invite' the Queen to land – a ceremony Her Majesty recalls with fondness

Once on land, the fairytale welcome went on. The Queen was offered and courageously accepted a drink of the local brew – 'kava' – in a coconut shell, and one evening she attended a state ball escorted by 200 'glistening torchbearers'. Before she left Fiji, she was also given a tour of the islands by flying boat.

The next stage of the Queen's 44,000-mile Commonwealth tour was a visit to Tonga. This was as exotic as it was lavish, described locally as 'the most notable occasion in the history of the islands' since no ruling British sovereign had ever been there before.

Tonga is one of those Commonwealth countries which has an indigenous monarch. The kingdom is made up of 169 volcanic islands and islets in the South-West Pacific. On the main island, the towering figure of Queen Salote of Tonga was there to greet the Queen and the Duke of Edinburgh. The ceremonial arch under which the British

A Tongan feast, lavish enough to test the resolve of an abstemious Queen

visitors passed had been designed by Queen Salote herself and, to non-stop Tongan dancing, the welcoming feast of 2000 pigs, duck, fish, lobster, crab, pineapple, water melon, yams, bananas and coconut went on through most of the evening.

The Queen never eats a great deal; in London a light breakfast and a one-course lunch might well be followed by a boiled egg for supper. But the peoples of the Commonwealth countries she visits naturally want to welcome her with feasts and banquets, and politeness demands that she sample all they offer. However, she does have to take particular care what she eats when she's abroad. Shell fish is definitely out and sea food in general is approached with caution. One head of state who gave a dinner in Her Majesty's honour says, 'The Queen does little more than pick at her food. But she does just enough never to cause offence. At her banquets one is entertained royally, but I would not say that food is her greatest passion.'

In between feasts in Tonga the Queen took pictures and Prince Philip went swimming in an atmosphere described at the time as a 'Polynesian delight, informal, unsophisticated and vivid'. The official record of the Queen's visit concluded: 'Queen Elizabeth looked as she must have felt – a young woman both relaxed and happy in the presence of the exotic delights that only the charm of Queen Salote can diffuse.'

On 23 December the *Gothic* docked in Auckland on the North Island of New Zealand, where the Royal visitors were given an ecstatic welcome. It was the first visit that any monarch had made to this most distant, most loyal

An enthusiastic welcome to New Zealand in 1953. It hasn't changed after thirty-three years

and most English dominion. It was also the first time that the Queen had spent Christmas away from her family, and she was to deliver her first Christmas Day broadcast after her Coronation in a Commonwealth country.

On Christmas morning itself, the Queen and the Duke of Edinburgh attended a service at the historic wooden cathedral church of St Mary, where the Duke read the second lesson. Before the service more than two hundred children had arrived at Government House, accompanied by Santa Claus and his sleigh drawn by six grey ponies. The children and Santa Claus had brought Christmas presents for Prince Charles and Princess Anne.

In the hall of Government House, there was a splendid Christmas tree and scarlet mistletoe from the slopes of Mount Tonagriro, hung with coloured streamers decorating all the rooms. Christmas dinner was traditional

The Queen's first Christmas away from home. It was 'rather strange,' she says, to see Father Christmas in summer

– turkey and plum pudding and Christmas crackers
flown out from London.

At nine that evening, on a mid-summer's night in New
Zealand, the Queen made her broadcast to the Commonwealth.

> As I travel across the world today, I am ever
> more deeply impressed with the achievement and
> the opportunity which the modern Common-
> wealth presents. Like New Zealand, from whose
> North Island I am speaking, every one of its
> nations can be justly proud of what it has built
> for itself on its own soil. But their greatest
> achievement, I suggest, is the Commonwealth
> itself, and that owes much to all of them.

This first Commonwealth tour had been heralded as
the dawn of a new Elizabethan age – 10,000 miles by
plane, 900 miles by car, 2500 miles by rail and the rest by
sea. What was really important to her, the Queen said,
was that she was beginning a journey 'in order to see as
much as possible of the people and countries of the
Commonwealth . . . to learn at first hand something of
their triumphs and difficulties and something of their
hopes and fears'. And Her Majesty went on to state what
has become for her the recurring and constant belief in
her Commonwealth role. 'At the same time,' she said, 'I
want to show that the Crown is not merely an abstract
symbol of our unity but a personal bond between you and
me.'

In this speech, made only six months after her
Coronation in Westminster Abbey, the new monarch set
out very clearly her hopes about how her reign would
develop. Over thirty years later, it is still a remarkable
testament to her faith in everything the Commonwealth
stands for today.

> Some people have expressed the hope that my
> reign may mark a new Elizabethan age. Frankly,
> I do not myself feel at all like my great Tudor
> forebear, who was blessed with neither husband
> nor children, who ruled as a despot and was

never able to leave these shores. But there is at least one significant resemblance between her age and mine. For her kingdom, small though it may have been and poor by comparison with her European neighbours, was yet great in spirit and well endowed with men who were ready to en-compass the earth. Now this great Common-wealth – of which I am so proud to be the Head, and of which that ancient kingdom forms a part – though rich in material resources is richer still in the enterprise and courage of its peoples.

The Queen then went on to speak about the fact that it would have been impossible for the adventurous heroes of Tudor and Stuart times to realise what would emerge and grow from the settlements they and later pioneers founded. 'From the Empire of which they built the frame, there has risen a worldwide fellowship of nations of a type never seen before.'

The Royal couple were greeted enthusiastically wherever they went in New Zealand, and nowhere was the welcome greater than when they were received on 2 January with traditional ancient ceremony by a huge crowd of Maoris at Rotorua. The men leapt, gesticulated and chanted in a ceremonial war dance, while the women performed graceful Maori dances. Both the Queen and the Duke were presented with and clad in ceremonial Kiwi feather cloaks. In her speech to them the Queen urged the Maoris to 'hold fast' to their own language and culture, and to their delight greeted them in their own tongue, 'Kiaora kou'tou'.

The most informal moment of the tour came when a four-year-old girl, Esther Fawcett, slipped away from her grandmother and walked boldly up the dais to see the Queen. There she stood, barefoot but bonneted. The Queen invited the child to sit beside her, and she sat there cross-legged throughout the ceremony.

History was made in Wellington when the Queen in her Coronation robes drove to open Parliament – the first time a sovereign had done so in New Zealand. It was described as 'the supreme event' of the whole visit.

The Queen leaving Parliament House in Adelaide, Australia after a state banquet

When she left New Zealand on 30 January 1954, Her
Majesty was reported to be visibly moved when she saw
the unbroken mass of thousands of people who turned up
to watch her departure.

*An Australian
address of welcome
to the Royal couple*

On 3 February she landed in Sydney, the first time a
reigning monarch had ever set foot on Australian soil.
There was another enthusiastic welcome, with decora-
tions and illuminations reputedly costing £2 million, but
the highlight of the Sydney visit was probably the surf
carnival at Bondi Beach, when the Queen and Prince
Philip watched in baking sunshine as the surfwaves
came crashing ashore.

In Canberra, the federal capital, the Queen – again
wearing her Coronation robes – opened a new session of
the Australian Parliament. At the Melbourne cricket
ground 17,000 children gathered to welcome the Queen.
At the town of Whyalla the Queen had a chance to watch
Aboriginal dances which had 'never before been seen by

a white woman', and in Queensland, a tiny four-year-old girl stole the show by trying to kiss the Queen. She managed to put her arms around the Queen's neck before the Queen, surprised but smiling, managed to 'disengage' her.

Paying her respects to a loyal naval escort. The Queen visits HMAS Australia

Getting accustomed to yet another Royal welcome, this time in the Cocos Islands

After a two-month stay in Australia the Royal party left on board the *Gothic* for the long journey home. It was by now 1 April 1954 and the Queen had already been away for four months.

Their first stop was in Ceylon, where once again she wore her magnificent Coronation gown to open Parliament. On this occasion, however, it was so hot that the glass beads on her dress heated up, and she recalls that it was 'like being in a radiator'. The Royal couple spent several days on the island, visiting the many splendid sights which Ceylon has to offer.

Then it was off again across the Indian Ocean to the British protectorate of Aden and, so that Africa should not feel omitted from the grand tour, the Royal couple paid a visit to Uganda to open a hydro-electric scheme at Owen Falls.

Opening parliament in Ceylon. The Queen remembers it as 'a complete contrast from Westminster . . . in an extraordinary hall open to the elements on each side'

Walking in the heat to a rock fortress in Ceylon. Her Majesty is thought to have lost weight on this part of the tour

The Queen and Prince Philip are shown ancient ruins in Ceylon

As they took off from Entebbe airport to fly north they were homeward bound at last, although it would be nearly six more weeks before they arrived in London. Off Tobruk on the North African coast a very special reunion took place. The young Prince Charles and his younger sister Anne had travelled out to see their parents for the first time in nearly six months. The Queen later joked of this reunion: 'They were extremely polite – I don't think they knew who we were at all!' The children had travelled out on the *Britannia*, which was making its maiden voyage to bring the Royal Family home.

The Royal couple love the *Britannia* dearly and the Queen constantly emphasises the invaluable role that

A rendezvous in Malta – Countess Mountbatten accompanies Her Majesty, now reunited with her children, towards the end of her round-the-world tour

the ship has played on Royal tours. It has made it possible for the Royal party to visit many small members of the Commonwealth in the Caribbean and South Pacific which could not possibly accommodate them otherwise. As the Queen said on *Britannia's* launch, 'My father felt most strongly, as I do, that a yacht was a necessity and not a luxury for the Head of our great Commonwealth, between whose countries the sea is no barrier, but the natural and indestructible highway.' And it is a great solace for Her Majesty to be able to retire to the privacy of the Royal yacht during the hectic programmes arranged for her.

On her maiden voyage, *Britannia* carried the Queen on the last stages of her triumphant round-the-world tour.

As she steamed towards Malta she was met by fifteen ships of the Mediterranean Fleet under the command of Prince Philip's uncle, Admiral of the Fleet Lord Mountbatten. Forming a sea-lane of two columns, each fired a salute of twenty-one guns as *Britannia* passed between them.

The visit to Malta must have brought back happy memories to the Queen of when she visited her husband 'as an ordinary officer's wife' during his service on HMS *Magpie*. The Royal tour made its last stop before home at Gibraltar, and her children took the glare of publicity off the Queen for a few moments as the press voraciously photographed them with the apes of Gibraltar.

At last, on 15 May 1954, *Britannia* sailed up the Thames through an open Tower Bridge to the Pool of London. The

Britannia comes up the Thames on the way home. The Queen remembers coming up 'this dirty commercial river' with Winston Churchill, who 'described it as the silver thread which runs through the history of Britain . . . he saw things in a very romantic and literary way'

Queen Mother and Princess Margaret boarded the yacht for a private reunion, and then they all travelled by barge to Westminster pier to be welcomed by the rest of the Royal Family.

But it was not only her family that met the young Queen. Hundreds of Londoners lined the banks of the Thames to greet her and Prince Philip after 'the greatest single journey ever undertaken by a British monarch'. Travelling over 44,000 miles in just under six months, her journey had taken in ten countries all with different relationships with Britain. Australia and New Zealand represented the old dominions; Ceylon had recently become independent but was still to declare itself a republic; Jamaica, Fiji, Uganda and even Tonga with its own monarch were still colonial dependencies of Britain.

Times were changing, however. In her first Christmas broadcast in 1952 the Queen had referred to the British Commonwealth and Empire. By the following year the word 'British' had gone. Her Majesty symbolises the transformation from Empire to Commonwealth because much of that change has taken place during her reign. As the British Prime Minister, Margaret Thatcher, says:

> It's important to remember that it's been during the Queen's reign that we have seen the great transformation from Empire to Commonwealth. When the Queen came to the throne in 1952 the old dominions, India and Pakistan had already become independent of course, but the really massive transition – all the African countries becoming independent – took place during the reign of the Queen.
>
> And the Queen has watched it all. . . . She's seen each country come to London and negotiate an independent constitution; she's seen them go from colony to nationhood, the move from Empire to Commonwealth. . . . So the Queen is in a unique position which is unlikely ever to be repeated in our history.

That first epic tour was remarkable, but it was only the first of many. To maintain the 'human links' it has been necessary to keep up the connection, and every country in the Commonwealth has been visited at least once by the Queen and Prince Philip.

The role of Prince Philip on these often long and arduous tours must not be underestimated. Where the Queen may nervously eye some local and strange-looking delicacy the Prince can be seen cheerfully tucking in with every appearance of enjoyment. And of course he has undertaken many tours of Commonwealth countries on his own.

Nor must one neglect to mention the other members of the Royal Family. Sometimes, many years may separate visits from the Queen to one of the Commonwealth countries, but it can be guaranteed that they will not have been forgotten in the meantime. At some point there will have been a visit from Princess Margaret, the Queen Mother, Princess Anne or 'Number one piccaninny bilong Mrs Quin' – as the Prince of Wales is known in Papua New Guinea.

CHAPTER 3

India and Asia

'This visit has shown that the new Commonwealth is firmly based in the hearts and minds of the people as a means of co-operation and the progress of mankind.'
HER MAJESTY THE QUEEN

On 21 January 1961, Her Majesty the Queen, accompanied by Prince Philip, stepped from her aeroplane into the brilliant sunshine at Delhi airport to begin a historic and memorable visit to India. It was the first visit by a British monarch since India and Pakistan had become independent nations – an event which had set in train the inexorable dissolution of the old British Empire and laid the foundations for the birth of the new Commonwealth.

Only fifty years before her visit, the British Empire was at its peak. When George V made his famous Delhi Durbar visit in 1911, India was still the glittering jewel in the glorious crown of Empire, and Viceroy Lord Curzon could only have been half exaggerating when he said at the beginning of the century, 'As long as we rule India, we are the greatest power in the world.'

The Delhi Durbar of 1911 was the apotheosis of the imperial presence, but George V was the first and last British monarch to be crowned Emperor in India. It all began to turn sour eight years later.

Towards the middle of April 1919, parts of the Indian state of Punjab erupted in a series of disturbances. Two years before, the Liberal Edwin Montagu, on becoming Secretary of State for India, had told the House of Commons that his aim was to create the conditions for what he called 'the progressive realisation of the responsible government in India as an integral part of the British Empire'. The plan to put that into effect was to give India some say in the running of its own affairs but to leave the ultimate responsibility in the hands of British ministers.

No amount of cosmetic adjustment could prevent the inescapable drive to independence, however, and in 1947 India and Pakistan both became independent. They remained within the Commonwealth as republics, no longer owing allegiance to the British Crown but willingly accepting King George VI as Head of the Commonwealth.

In the debate in the British Parliament which preceded Indian independence, Winston Churchill and other diehard Tories of the imperial school had attacked the Attlee government for 'throwing away the Empire' in giving India her freedom. But in his 1948 Christmas broadcast, King George VI had asserted that Indian independence had had the opposite effect. It had strengthened the Commonwealth by extending independence to the new states of Asia. 'Our Commonwealth,' the King had said then, 'has been subject to the laws of evolution. But it is stronger, not weaker, as it fulfils its ancient mission of widening the bounds of freedom wherever our people live; and, for myself, I am proud to fulfil my own appointed share in that mission.'

When his daughter came down the steps of her aircraft in 1961, she said: 'I am thrilled to be here. To all India, I bring a greeting of goodwill and affection from the people of Britain.'

This visit, much more so than any other, was to be a stern test of Her Majesty as the 'human link' holding the Commonwealth together. She firmly believes that her visits to Commonwealth countries are concrete evidence of that human link, and in India in 1961 she was greeted at Delhi airport as head of the 'greatest democracy in the world' and of 'the great Commonwealth'.

The success of the Queen's visit to India exceeded even the wildest expectations. Two million people turned out to greet her on the drive through the streets of Delhi, and hundreds of thousands saw her lay a wreath on the memorial to Mahatma Gandhi – widely interpreted as

A warm welcome for the Queen in 1961 as she drives through the streets of Delhi with magnificent state pageantry. Two million people crowded into a route barely half a mile long to watch the procession

the final healing of an old wound. The Queen and the Duke rode on elephants to a reception in Jaipur, and attended scores of receptions and banquets and gala evenings. The Mayor of Delhi, speaking at a civic reception for the Royal couple and quoting from a classical Indian poet, solemnly intoned the age-old greeting: 'May you live a thousand years and may each year consist of fifty thousand days.'

It was impossible to ignore the fact that part of the Queen's first-ever visit to India coincided with three days of 'Republic Day' celebrations. At the Republic Day parade, where the Indian President took the salute, the Queen and the Duke of Edinburgh remained in the background. They took no salutes, the British national anthem was never played, and there were no Union Jacks

*Nehru insisted on
India becoming a
republic, but he kept
India in the
Commonwealth
and struck up a
close relationship
with the Queen*

A sombre moment on the 1961 tour of India – a visit to Gandhi's tomb

to greet them. But the Mayor of Delhi summed up the mood of his countrymen perfectly when, referring to relations between Britain and India during the run-up to independence, he spoke of a 'long history of conflict'. But he added, 'That conflict was ended in a unique manner honourable to both our country and yours. The evidence of the welcome we give you is far greater than the words

Royal continuity. The Queen floating down the Ganges on a ceremonial barge used by King George V

used in this address. That evidence is spread out all around us.'

Evidence there was indeed. More than 400,000 people listened to the Mayor of Delhi's speech. From Delhi, the Queen went to Agra to see the famous Taj Mahal, and to the picturesque lakeside city of Udaipur for a picnic lunch and a leisurely cruise on the lake.

Pausing among the lakes and gardens of the Taj Mahal

An elevated view for Her Majesty – atop an elephant

On a flying visit to Pakistan, the riotous greeting given to the Royal couple by hundreds of thousands of people in Ahmedabad were proof enough that there was no legacy of bitterness left from the communal strife and bloodshed which had accompanied Pakistan's independ-

A stop on the way to the famous Khyber Pass

ence. One million people lined the streets of Karachi, shouting, 'Long live the Queen'. Accorded a lavish welcome in Peshawar, the Queen was moved to say, 'It seems to me that the Pakistanis and the British have a common talent for pageantry.'

Then it was back to India and to Calcutta. Along a five-mile route there was hardly a roadside space, a cranny or a building that could possibly have held another person, and the crush of people threatened to overwhelm the progress of the Royal party. In such crowds carefully timed schedules come under heavy strain, and sometimes delay is unavoidable.

There have been many times when Her Majesty has gone out of her way to ease the obvious embarrassment of latecomers to her functions. On one such occasion her Indian guests arrived late because their cars had been prevented from arriving on time by a jam of bullock-drawn carts. When the Indian politicians eventually arrived – steaming under the collar in the afternoon heat and terribly uneasy at being so late – the Queen calmly turned the conversation to the weather in England and

A Valentine Day gift for the Queen from the children of Dhaka in 1961

commented on reports she had heard about snow on the ground at Sandringham. It was a brilliant attempt to 'cool down' her guests, as one Indian leader later put it.

She has a tremendous sense of humour, and there is a mischievous side to her nature. She enjoys seeing little things go wrong and, because she herself is always correct but never pompous, she relishes those occasions when her powerful and important politicians fail to get their arrangements just right.

In her farewell speech to India, which was translated into fifteen dialects and broadcast nationwide, the Queen said: 'This visit has shown that the new Commonwealth is firmly based in the hearts and minds of the people as a means of co-operation and the progress of mankind.'

All the turbulence and political agitation which preceded India's independence were forgotten in the warmth of the Queen's visit, and one Indian commentator said:

People are frequently amazed that the people of India can still, after all that happened, retain such an affection and indeed a great love for the British. Part of the answer of course is that, for better or worse, we have shared a part of history. At a significant time in our development, and I mean in both our developments, our lives . . . crossed. And whether one likes it or not, that fact cannot be disregarded.

Unlike some other great powers, Britain realised that you cannot hold on to a people or a country without its consent. And Britain was forced to concede our independence. But we were left with certain internationally marketable traditions: the British parliamentary system, our love for democracy, English law and of course the language itself.

Modern India has been able to use these assets to further . . . our own development in our own way. But we owe it to the British and we love them for it. And when we see the Queen we think of what she represents and about the Commonwealth in which we know she believes. In Her Majesty, there is a bridge between the old and the new. She is that symbol. She sees herself as that unifying force and we respect that and love her for it.

The Queen's 1961 visit to India confirmed her own devout and personal faith in the ideals of the Commonwealth. She had seen the new India – no longer part of the Empire, but a member of the multi-racial, multinational Commonwealth of nations. The following year in her Christmas message, the Queen made a special reference to the relationship between the older members of the Commonwealth, like Canada, and the newer members like India:

The feeling of a special relationship between the ordinary people of the older Commonwealth countries will never be weakened. This feeling is rapidly spreading throughout the newer members, and in its turn will help us realise the ideal of human brotherhood.

In the ideal of the Commonwealth, we have been entrusted with something very special. We

have in our hands a most potent force for good
and one of the true unifying bonds in this torn
world. Let us keep faith with the ideal we know
to be right, and be ambitious for the good of all
men.

*A glittering state
banquet*

*Local women dis-
play pottery to the
Queen in a village
just outside Delhi*

It was twenty-two years before the Queen was to visit the
sub-continent again. The Royal tour in the autumn of
1983 had started in Kenya, where she had re-visited
Treetops – the safari hotel at which she had first learned
of her accession to the throne on the death of her father in
1952.

After three days in Kenya she went on for her first visit
to Bangladesh, which, with over 95 million people, is the
second most populated country in the Commonwealth.
The Queen has always been very conscious that, apart
from Britain and the three white dominions, the rest of
the Commonwealth consists of some of the world's
poorest nations. The plight of Bangladesh is among the
gravest.

Bangladesh was formerly East Pakistan – one half of
the unnatural amalgam of Muslim people separated by
the entire width of Hindu India. After the final rift had
come between the two Pakistans in 1971, Bangladesh
immediately applied to join the Commonwealth and was
accepted in 1972. It was a situation not acceptable to
Pakistan and she withdrew from the association.

On this, her first visit, the Queen came face to face with
poverty as she took the hand of a starving child at a Save

*Coming face to face
with poverty in the
Commonwealth.
The Queen re-
marked on the
'widening gap' be-
tween the rich and
poor in her 1983
Christmas Broad-
cast after this visit
to Bangladesh,
when she met baby
Jamal*

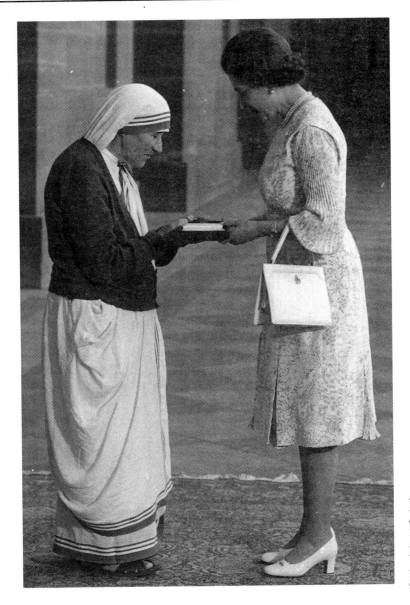

A presentation of the Honorary Order of Merit to Mother Teresa of Calcutta. Her Majesty was very impressed by her work among the poor of India

the Children centre in Dhaka. The child was two years old but looked much younger, with arms like matchsticks and legs so thin that they could fit into glove fingers. His weary brown eyes were pitiful enough to attract the attention of the Queen who, in thirty-one years of travelling, had trained herself not to get too emotionally involved. But when little Jamal put his arms out, the Queen's response was immediate. Afterwards she said she was 'moved and impressed' by what she had seen, and she told Jamal, 'I will tell my daughter to come and visit you.' The happy postscript to this particular story is that when Princess Anne, as President of the Save the Children Fund, visited the centre three months later she found a healthy, growing child.

The Queen arrived in Delhi on 17 November to be greeted at the airport by both the President of India and Mrs Indira Gandhi, the Prime Minister. Hindu astrologers brought about a change in the Queen's programme by announcing that the scheduled time of her arrival, promptly at noon, was inauspicious. Accordingly, the Queen arrived at five minutes past noon instead. A Hindu demonstration forced the Queen to postpone the laying of a wreath at Gandhi's shrine, but she visited Hyderabad, where her wedding anniversary weekend began rather unromantically with a visit to a factory manufacturing steam-turbine machinery. The Duke in the meantime went to a game reserve for a ride on an elephant.

Then they both went on to a visit to Poona, where high in the hills the Queen reviewed cadets of the Indian services in a ceremony little changed from the days of the Raj. But up in the hills, where British wives once took their children away from the heat of the plains, it was no cooler: the air shimmered at 100 degrees and the parade ground looked hazy.

Back in Delhi, much of the splendour of the British Raj had been recreated for the visit. The Queen and Prince Philip were staying in the former Viceregal Palace as guests of the President, and there they were attended by bearers in sparkling white and red liveries and turbans, much as their forebears had been seventy years before when the Queen's grandfather, George V, came to Delhi for his coronation as Emperor of India. The suite where the Royal couple stayed had been completely redecorated in the style of the Raj. And in New Delhi, the Queen conducted perhaps her strangest-ever walkabout. It was in a palanquin, the traditional bride's canopy. At first the Queen looked bemused to find she was expected to actually walk along inside this 'love bus', but after only a

The Queen and Mrs Indira Gandhi talked a great deal about Third World poverty

moment's hesitation she stepped in and began her walkabout, to the delight of the crowds.

At a state banquet hosted by the Indian Prime Minister, Mrs Gandhi, the Queen spoke of the new bond that had been forged between India and Britain:

> We share a wealth of common values and interests . . . a devotion to democratic ideals and to the institutions which maintain them, strong industrial and commercial links, and in Britain today a thriving community of people of Indian origin who make such a full contribution to our national life.

The memory of this tour was fresh in her mind when she said in her 1983 Christmas broadcast that 'in spite of all the progress that has been made the greatest problem in the world today remains the gap between rich and poor countries'. Although there were objections in some quarters in Britain to this remark on the grounds that it was 'political', there was little doubt elsewhere that these were no idle words. She had been and seen for herself and she was entitled to speak out.

Mrs Gandhi had been proud to host the 1983 Commonwealth heads of government meeting in Delhi, but it was the last time that most of her Commonwealth colleagues were to see her alive. On 31 October 1984 she was struck down by Sikh assassins, who were part of her own bodyguard, as she walked in the early morning sun through the garden of her home.

World leaders were shocked. The Queen sent a private message of sympathy to Mrs Gandhi's eldest son, Rajiv, who was to succeed her as leader of the 750 million people of India. The Queen's public message of condolence was sent to President Singh and said: 'The world and the Commonwealth have lost one of their most distinguished leaders.'

The Queen was represented at the funeral by Princess Anne, who was in India in her capacity as President of the Save the Children Fund. Many Commonwealth leaders – among them Kenneth Kaunda, Milton Obote and Robert Mugabe – attended the funeral. All the leaders of the British political parties went and the Prime Minister, Mrs Thatcher, added a personal note: 'For my part I shall feel greatly the loss of a wise colleague and personal friend. I always looked forward to our talks together – they had some special quality and understanding.' In the House of Commons she said that Mrs Gandhi's death 'had robbed the Commonwealth of a statesman of outstanding stature and experience'.

Only twelve months after the tragic death of his mother, the 41-year-old Rajiv was to attend his first Commonwealth heads of government meeting. With his quiet, persuasive charm, he and the equally charming newcomer Brian Mulroney of Canada were to play the key roles in arriving at a Commonwealth consensus over South African sanctions. In eleventh-hour talks at the weekend retreat at Lyford Cay, Mulroney and Gandhi came to an agreement with Mrs Thatcher which enabled the Secretary-General, Sonny Ramphal, to announce a Commonwealth accord. It had been a close-run thing, as Ramphal later confessed, but Commonwealth unity had been maintained – and it was in no small way due to Rajiv Gandhi and Brian Mulroney.

Many years ago, Lord Curzon recognised that without India the British Empire had no real strength, and it is equally certain that without India's continual support the Commonwealth would be similarly weakened. Fortunately for all, Rajiv Gandhi is a firm supporter of the Commonwealth ideal. He feels it is 'an association that brings countries together . . . a melting pot of ideas. One of the biggest advantages of the Commonwealth is that we all speak English. . . . It is of relevance not just to India but to the world.'

Overshadowed in size by its giant neighbour, Sri Lanka – the island at the foot of the Indian sub-continent – is nevertheless equally enthusiastic about the Commonwealth. After all, it was India, Pakistan and Ceylon that were the first non-white members of the new Commonwealth, joining in 1948. The country changed its name to Sri Lanka in 1978, and became a republic. The Queen first visited Ceylon on her memorable round-the-world tour of 1954, and she returned in 1961 and 1981.

Further east from the sub-continent is the post-colonial creation of Malaysia which, like Topsy, just grew and grew. British interests in this part of Asia had largely been associated with trade and the protection of strategic trade routes. In 1948 Malaya consisted of nine individual states ruled by sultans, which, with Singapore, were known as the Strait Settlements. After a bitterly fought jungle war between British troops and Communist guerrillas, Malaya became independent in 1957 under the rule of Tunku Abdul Rahman. Singapore became separately independent in 1965, followed by

Britain's other interests in the area, Sarawak and North
Borneo (now Sabah).

These four states joined together and became Malaysia
in September 1963, but the association was not to last
long in that form. Tunku Abdul Rahman and the wily,
tough leader of Singapore, Lee Kuan Yew, were fundamentally different characters and, though both were
vigorously anti-communist, they could not agree on
other matters and Singapore left the federation two
years later.

*A visit to a rubber
plantation in
Malaysia, 1972*

Lee Kuan Yew is still Prime Minister of Singapore and
is one of the elder statesmen of the Commonwealth. He
hosted the Commonwealth heads of government meeting in 1971 and, although the Queen was not in
attendance for this meeting, they have had plenty of
occasions on which to get to know each other well. He
says of the Queen's role as Head of the Commonwealth,
'She's symbolic. . . . We share a certain experience which

makes us understand each other and she represents that continuity and change.'

Malaysia's Prime Minister is now Dr Mahathir Mohamed and, although his acquaintance with the Commonwealth is shorter, he too is impressed with the Queen's grasp of Commonwealth issues. 'It's easy talking to her and if I talk to her about my country I feel that she knows what I'm talking about. That's very impressive for a person who has to meet forty-nine different leaders.'

The Queen's only tour of South-East Asia and the Indian Ocean Territories was as far back as 1972, but it illustrated her determination to visit at some time all the countries of the Commonwealth, however remote.

The tour started in Bangkok, the spectacular capital of Thailand. From Bangkok the Royal party, which included not only the Duke of Endinburgh but also Princess Anne, sailed in *Britannia* to Malaysia. Kuala Lumpur, the capital and government centre of the Malaysian Federation, had changed little since its days as the administrative centre of the Malay States. Then it was a thriving centre for rubber and tin production, where British planters sweated in the equatorial heat before returning to their bungalow for gin slings on the verandah. Malaya was the epitome of the old colonial way of life.

From Malaya the Royal party visited the remote territories of Sarawak and Sabah, where they were greeted by members of the former head-hunting Murut tribe who stood guard with six-foot blowpipes.

It was on this tour that the Queen visited the Sultanate of Brunei. Under a treaty made in 1888, the Sultanate became a British protectorate; this meant that, while the Sultan had control over domestic matters, Britain kept a firm control over its defence and external affairs and it was not until 1 January 1984 that Brunei became a fully sovereign and independent state. Brunei is at the time of writing the most recent country to join the Commonwealth, and the Sultan is one of the five indigenous monarchs of a Commonwealth country.

HM Sultan Hassanal Bolkiah is the twenty-ninth of his line to succeed to the throne and is reputed to be one of the world's richest men. The oil-rich Sultan is said to have an annual income of £2.7 billion and, to celebrate his independence from Britain, he built himself a palace three times the size of Buckingham Palace at an estimated cost of £300–500 million. It sprawls across 300 landscaped acres and its 2 million square feet of floor space accommodate 1788 sumptuously decorated rooms. To achieve this splendour a tropical rain forest was felled, a mountain top was decapitated and 4 million tons of earth were removed.

The Sandhurst-educated Sultan also owns more than 100 cars, a yacht and his own Boeing 727. But despite his fabulous wealth and his many properties all over the world, the Sultan is not known as a jet-setting playboy. He takes his duties seriously and leads a devout Muslim life. In Brunei he also holds the position of prime minister, finance minister and home affairs minister.

After leaving Singapore and Malaysia the Royal tour of 1972 continued across the Indian Ocean. After four days at sea *Britannia* arrived in the Maldive Islands, a collection of tiny islands that stretch for 200 miles. They

The state opening of Parliament in Mauritius, 1972

were never a British colony but, like other states in the region, the country had its own sultan and came under British protection. In 1965 the islands became completely independent, but it was not until 1982 that they joined the Commonwealth – at first as a special member. Special membership of the Commonwealth is reserved for very small states. It gives them the right to participate in all functional meetings and activities, but does not entitle them to attend full heads of government meetings. The Maldives were granted full Commonwealth status in 1985, and now only Nauru and Tuvalu remain as special members.

Two more former British dependencies and recent members of the Commonwealth were visited on this tour, the Seychelles and Mauritius. In spending two or three days in these tiny states the Queen showed how seriously she believes that she must be *seen* as Head of the Commonwealth.

The Queen adding the final touches to a dragon's make-up for Chinese New Year celebrations in the New Territories, Hong Kong, 1975

CHAPTER 4

Australasia

'People in my country feel the Queen represents the
common bond that holds us together . . . people see in
her someone who is above tribal loyalty and conflict.'
MICHAEL SOMARE *Former Prime Minister, Papua New Guinea*

Australia had never been visited by a reigning monarch
until the Queen arrived in Sydney on 3 Feburary 1954. It
was an important visit, designed to strengthen a
relationship with Britain and the Commonwealth which
has not always been smooth. How well the Queen did on
that first trip and on others later on can be judged by the
fact that the relationship with this Commonwealth
member has survived the dismissal of an Australian
prime minister by the Queen's representative, the
Governor-General, and the fact that the republican
voices which were once so prominent are now less so.

A British settlement from the late eighteenth century,
subsequently a colony, then a dominion, Australia now
consists of the six former colonies of New South Wales,
Victoria, South Australia, Queensland, Western Australia and Tasmania. With the three other 'old white'
Commonwealth countries, Australia gained sovereignty
from Britain under the terms of the Statute of Westminster in 1931. The Queen is represented as head of state by
a Governor-General who is appointed on the advice of
the Australian Prime Minister, and in 1974 Her Majesty
adopted the style and title of the Queen of Australia.

Australia's relationship with Britain has always been
important, but unequal. During the depression, Australia was weighed down by interest charges on debts which

came mainly from British sources. The country's economy was closely tied to Britain's, and that fact disrupted all domestic attempts in Australia to diversify its trade. There were also political problems related to the degree of control that the British government had over the country.

After the Second World War, however, came a movement which has been described as 'the greening of Australia'. The country was developing a sense of its own identity as an independent nation, and no longer relied so heavily on Britain. Both Australia and New Zealand began a creative policy of forging closer links with the countries of their own region, including states like Japan and Indonesia as well as those of the Commonwealth.

A spectacular arrival in Sydney, Australia, 1954 – the first time a reigning monarch had ever set foot on Australian soil

An additional factor in this increasing feeling of independence was the fact that (although the population of Australia is still predominantly of British stock, apart from the approximately 160,000 Aborigines) there has been a large inflow of immigrants from Eastern, Central and Southern Europe, and from the Middle East, since the war. These new Australians have had some effect in changing the fundamentally British character of the country – Greeks, Poles and Yugoslavs do not display the same attachment to Britain as the old mother country.

Nevertheless, the Queen has always been greatly loved by Australians, and in 1954 she commanded crowds of a third of a million people at the Sydney Cricket Ground. She was a glamorous figure, the mother of two young children, and the country took her to their hearts. Since then she has visited Australia frequently, taking Prince Charles and Princess Anne with her in 1970 and returning in 1973 to open the Sydney Opera House. She and Prince Philip made a major tour of Australia, New Zealand and the Commonwealth countries of the South Pacific in her Silver Jubilee year, and she visited Melbourne for the Commonwealth heads of government meeting in 1981, and Brisbane for the Commonwealth Games in 1982.

During her visits in the 1970s, Her Majesty ran headlong into the stirrings of Australian republicanism. From time to time it has been fashionable to talk of the country becoming a republic, and after the Labour party gained power in 1972 the designated High Commissioner to London declared that it was a certainty. But the Labour leaders and their supporters were only 'long-term' republicans, believing that a republic of Australia would probably not be proclaimed in their lifetime, but maybe in their children's time. So no concrete proposals to make Australia a republic were made. This indefinite state of affairs continued until November 1975, when the Governor-General Sir John Kerr dismissed the Labour Prime Minister Gough Whitlam and his government, appointing Malcolm Fraser as 'caretaker'. He did this because the country was facing a constitutional crisis

*Something typically
Australian – a surf
carnival!*

after the government had been refused money by the Senate, and Gough Whitlam would not resign.

Although Sir John Kerr's actions were bound by the Australian constitution, the Queen was dragged into a highly charged debate and the flames of republicanism were re-kindled. Her Majesty could only reply that she was constitutionally bound not to interfere with the Governor-General's tenure of office 'except upon advice from the Australian Prime Minister'. Alarmed by such a fervent display of republicanism, the London *Times* suggested that Sir John Kerr should be superseded by none other than Prince Charles. That has not come about and doesn't now seem very likely.

Today, though there are some minor displays of republicanism on some of the Queen's visits, most Australians do not criticise the Queen personally and believe that she is 'hard-working and well-meaning'. Indeed, an American magazine which took the trouble and time to research Australian republicanism found that the monarchy's popularity rating had dropped only

a fraction in the past dozen years. However, the press
does not always get it right, and after the Silver Jubilee
tour of Australia the Queen made it known that she was
extremely displeased with wildly exaggerated reports of
minor demonstrations. For example, a thin card claim-
ing 'Independence for Australia' which had been thrown
into the Royal car became, in the next day's papers, the
heavy placard which could have concussed the Queen.

*A children's rally in
Adelaide*

When he was in opposition, Bob Hawke said at
a party given for the media in Melbourne: 'The Queen is a
decent hard-working lady doing a useful job, but by the
end of the century the monarchy will be phased out, not
to mention the expense of the tour.' But today Mr Hawke,
in the political driving-seat as Prime Minister, is not so
sure. He still believes that his country might one day
become a republic, but is sure that it will always
remain in the Commonwealth.

But it's not something I'm pushing, it's not something which is an issue today. I've made the point
before now, that if Australia were to become a
republic overnight like that, it wouldn't change
anything for its people in real terms. It's the sort

of change which might eventually be made, but not necessarily now; perhaps some time in the future.

One change that has been made, however, is that the last outdated legal fetters tying Australia to Britain have recently been removed. The Judicial Committee of the Privy Council in London is no longer the final court of appeal for Australians, and the Westminster Parliament now has no control whatsoever over Australia. Such powers as it did have have not been exercised for many years, but nevertheless the London *Times* proclaimed that Australia was 'independent at last'.

The Queen placed this new relationship between Australia and Britain on a formal footing in a speech at Parliament House in Canberra on 3 March 1986. She said:

I can see a growing sense of identity and a fierce pride in being Australian. So it is right that the Australia Act has finally severed the last of the constitutional links between Australia and Britain, and I was glad to play a dual role in this. My last official action as Queen of the United Kingdom before leaving London last month was to give my Assent to the Australia Act from the Westminster Parliament. My first official action on arriving in Australia yesterday was to proclaim an identical Act – but from the Australian Parliament – which I did as Queen of Australia. Surely no two independent countries could bring to an end their constitutional relationship in a more civilised way, and I hope you will agree with me that this has been symbolic of the depth and quality of the relationship between Australia and Britain. Anachronistic constitutional arrangements have disappeared – but the friendship between two nations has been strengthened and will endure.

Having at one time criticised the expense of Her Majesty's tours abroad, the Prime Minister now has this to say about the role of the Queen in the Commonwealth.

Speaking as Bob Hawke and also as Prime Minister of Australia, I can put it this way. I have had the opportunity now of meeting Her Majesty on many occasions. I think she has arguably got the most difficult job in the world. I think she discharges it with an absolutely remarkable capacity and composure, commitment and dedication, relieved by what I find is a magnificent sense of humour.

Australians know that sense of humour well. During the Queen's 1981 visit a photographer at one of her parties aboard the Royal yacht dropped his glass of sherry at her feet and, to his horror, watched it spread itself liberally across what had been an unblemished carpet. Her Majesty continued her conversation, almost as if she had not noticed what had happened. But several hours later, at a different engagement, the same man dropped one of his cameras at the Queen's feet as she was about to be greeted by her hosts. It made a frightful clatter, and there was an embarrassing silence before the Queen roared with laughter and said to the photographer, 'Oh dear! It just really hasn't been your day', at which point there was general light-hearted laughter at the incident.

But the unfortunate photographer could take comfort from the fact that, some years before, Her Majesty had been forced to change her dress when a nervous guest spilled his sherry near her. And it remains a source of amusement to the Queen that many people who would prefer a large scotch or a brandy always choose sherry at her parties. 'What a lot of sherry drinkers!' she says, holding her glass of tonic water elegantly.

There have also been memorable moments of Royal informality on Australian tours. A former Australian Prime Minister, John Gorton, recalls that on the Queen's bi-centenary visit in 1970, while the Royal yacht was anchored near one of the islands off the Great Barrier

Reef, someone decided that everyone should be thrown in the water. It got so out of hand that Mr Gorton almost threw the Queen into the sea.

> Princess Anne was thrown in and then Prince Philip. I was sitting next to Her Majesty and I was just about to throw her in, but I looked at her and something about the way she looked at me told me that perhaps I shouldn't. In the end, the Queen was the only one who stayed dry.

The Prince of Wales has also played a crucial part in cementing the relationship between Australia and Britain. He has visited Australia, New Zealand and other Commonwealth countries in the area nineteen times since his first visit at the end of January 1966, when he spent part of the school year as an exchange student at Geelong Grammar School in Melbourne. The visit was intended to ensure that Charles got to know his Commonwealth, and by all accounts it was a success. Although he hated leaving home he later admitted that he 'absolutely adored' his time there. He said, 'In Australia there is no such thing as an aristocracy or anything like it. . . . You are judged there on how people feel about you.'

By all accounts people felt pretty happy about him when he took his new bride and infant son, Prince William, on a four-week tour of Australia in 1983. The Princess of Wales insisted that she was not to be parted from baby William at such an important stage in his development, so baby and nanny were added to the Royal entourage. In years to come Prince William can truly claim that he was the youngest member of the Royal Family ever to visit a Commonwealth country.

Contrary to popular belief, the first European to set sight of New Zealand was a Dutchman in the employ of the Dutch East India Company in 1642. The islands were named Niew Zeeland after a Dutch province and, although the ship's crew did not land, they thought the inhabitants hostile and the land poor.

The next visitor, over a century later, was Captain Cook in 1769. Cook found the indigenous population generally more friendly, and his warm reports of good harbours and the abundance of seals, timber and flax attracted the attention of sealers and traders. Among the first settlers were missionaries from New South Wales, whose aim was to assist the Maoris and introduce European farming. But the arrival of more traders, settlers and sailors, who generally lacked an established administration and rule of law at that time, caused much friction with the Maori population, whose traditional way of life began to break down under the impact of association with the Europeans.

At first the British government was reluctant to face up to these problems, and it was not until 1840 that a Lieutenant-Governor arrived on the islands with instructions to treat the Maoris as an independent nation, and negotiate with them as such. He quickly set about organising a meeting of chiefs, and on 6 February of that year forty-six Chiefs signed the Treaty of Waitangi, ceding sovereignty to Queen Victoria in return for the protection of the Crown. Despite this there was much friction between the indigenous population and the settlers, which resulted in the Maori Wars from 1860 to 1872. However, in the meantime a relatively straightforward governmental system was created by the British; New Zealand was given Dominion status in 1907 and was a founding member of the Statute of Westminster in 1931, although this was not adopted in the country until 1947.

New Zealand has always had a close identity with the Commonwealth and with Britain, and this goes a long way to explaining why the Queen has always enjoyed her visits to that country. On her first visit in 1953 she was greeted with enormous enthusiasm in Auckland, where the tour began. On the day after their arrival the Queen and Prince Philip went to the races, accompanied by 50,000 Aucklanders who turned up to see them, and Her Majesty's appearance at a film première was billed as the city's most glittering social occasion of all time. Her Majesty was described as the embodiment of youth and

dignity, and newspapers were united in proclaiming that the country had fallen in love 'with Her Gracious Majesty and her Royal Consort'.

The informality which characterises so many of the Queen's meetings with the peoples of the Commonwealth is demonstrated by a story she herself tells. On a visit to a youth rally during this first tour, she came upon two small girls who were having a lively argument about whether she or Princess Margaret was the Queen. Unable to resist the impulse, the Queen leaned over and said, 'No, it's me!'

The atmosphere is always totally relaxed during the Queen's visits to New Zealand, and it was this country that was chosen for the Queen's first 'walkabout' in Wellington in 1970. On Her Majesty's seventh visit in 1981, one New Zealander remarked, 'I think she feels very much at home here' – and this is clearly true.

Children greet the Queen on a journey through New Zealand's picturesque west coast on her first visit in 1954

*After the demon-
stration – an
explanation about
sheep-shearing in
New Zealand*

*The Queen with Sir
Keith Holyoake
after the state open-
ing of parliament in
Wellington, 1963*

*A sea of union flags
greets the Queen in
New Zealand*

Her Majesty talks to Maoris, wearing the ceremonial feather cloak which was presented to her on her first visit

The Queen has always felt a close bond of sympathy with the Maori inhabitants of the islands, and in January 1954 she was received by an enormous crowd at Rotorua with traditional Maori greetings and ceremony. The Royal couple were then presented with ceremonial cloaks which the Queen still wears on visits. Her second visit in 1961 coincided with Waitangi Day Celebrations, as it was the 123rd anniversary of the signing of the Treaty of Waitangi. Maoris warmly welcomed the Queen and she spoke a few words of Maori in her reply.

On her 1981 visit she was accorded the rare Polynesian greeting 'Te kotuku rarenga tahi', which loosely translated means 'Welcome, rare white heron of singular flight'. Quite what she made of that is unrecorded, but she smiled. Later, in the middle of a formal Maori address, the Queen and the Duke of Edinburgh roared with laughter when the speaker predicted that Prince Charles was about to make them grandparents again. The Maori speaker was remarkably accurate in his prediction – eighteen days later, Buckingham Palace announced that the Princess of Wales was pregnant.

By 1986 the Maori connection with the Queen had become rather more controversial, however. Soon after the Queen and Prince Philip arrived in February, two supporters of Maori rights were arrested for trying to attract publicity for their cause by throwing eggs at the Royal car, one of which hit the Queen and left a mark on her coat. This incident much embarrassed the Prime Minister, David Lange, who called it 'deplorable and unacceptable' behaviour and apologised to the Queen. The following day a Maori was arrested for baring his bottom, though the Queen did not see him. Then, just twenty-four hours later, a well-known Maori activist was arrested for attempting to join the Queen's motorcade, and later in Christchurch several Maori women bared their bottoms. Throughout the visit there were small bands of noisy protesters waving placards with 'Go home, Liz' on them, and although the Queen was certainly visibly shocked by the egg-throwing incident she was undeterred. At a banquet later she even joked that she preferred her New Zealand eggs for breakfast.

For all the attention the protestors have attracted, it would be a mistake to assume that New Zealand – one of the most ardently Royalist countries – is turning against the Queen. As one commentator said, the demonstrators were usually a very small group representing fringe political movements, and were not so much protesting about the Queen personally but drawing attention to their cause. David Lange was reported to be 'testy' at the coverage the incidents received in Britain, and told British journalists, 'She is the Queen of New Zealand. I don't remember complaining when a man got into her bedroom at Buckingham Palace. I wish you would look after her as well as we do in New Zealand.'

He is keen to stress the important role played by Her Majesty, with regard both to his own country and to the effectiveness of the Commonwealth as an organisation.

> The Commonwealth actually draws people together to take a hard look at the real plight of others. . . . It's because of its intimacy, its shared tradition and because of the simple fact that you regard the Queen as somehow the symbolic head of this collective organisation that some people change their views, their position.
>
> That explains this whole concept of Commonwealth consensus. Consensus in this sense doesn't mean that all Commonwealth countries must agree and be unanimous. Consensus means that the minority must not bully the majority by having a selfish or a small perspective. And it also means that the majority must say to those in a minority: 'We respect you; we respect your views. If you could move a little closer our way, we could start moving towards you.'

The Queen carried shoulder-high by local warriors on her arrival in Cook Island, 1974

Despite the distance, the Royal Family do not experience any great culture shock on their tours of Australia and New Zealand. The latter country particularly, with its gentle landscape and equally gentle climate, is often said to be more English than England. But in the Pacific there are several former British dependencies which are now members of the Commonwealth, and their customs and culture are very different.

Fiji became independent in 1970, when Prince Charles represented the Queen at the ceremony. Her Majesty is also head of state in three other Pacific states: the Solomon Islands, Tuvalu and Papua New Guinea.

Tuvalu was formerly administered jointly with its neighbour Kiribati as the Gilbert and Ellice Islands. It is, with Nauru, the smallest independent state in the Commonwealth – both have only 8000 inhabitants. They are so small that they are not represented at the heads of government meetings, and are accorded special membership of the Commonwealth.

The Queen is carried in a decorated canoe on her visit to Tuvalu in 1982. She described it as an 'unusual sensation'

The visit that the Queen made to the tiny island of Tuvalu in 1982 is one neither she nor the media are likely to forget. The press were astonished as they were presented with some of the most marvellous pictures they are ever likely to take on a Royal tour. The Queen, looking at first somewhat apprehensive, was carried ashore and through the streets in a large canoe, borne by garlanded islanders. Prince Philip, clearly enjoying every minute of it, came a little way behind in a second one.

The Queen feels that the people of the Pacific have 'a particular feeling of friendship. I suppose being islanders they always welcome strangers, and this was certainly an occasion when we were made very welcome.' She particularly appreciated the fact that 'all the people carrying the canoe and the ladies dancing, [who] are all civil servants and teachers normally, had . . . dressed so magnificently in their traditional clothes'.

Kiribati, Nauru, Vanuatu and Western Samoa are all republics, but the island of Tonga has maintained its own monarchy. Today, the monarch is King Taufa'ahau Tupou IV, whose mother was the large and cheerful Queen Salote who nearly stole the show at the Queen's coronation in 1953, as she rode in her open carriage in the rain.

A quizzical look at
an old friend – a
tortoise supposedly
presented to the
King of Tonga by
Captain Cook

A roast pig is borne
to the table for the
Jubilee feast in
Samoa, 1977

The Queen shares
a joke with her
Samoan host

The Queen with the
King of Tonga. Her
Majesty feels par-
ticularly at home
among the 'friendly
island' people of the
South Pacific

The largest Commonwealth member of this group is
Papua New Guinea, and its story is by far the strangest.
Papua New Guinea was never a British colony in the
strictest sense of the word but had been a dependency of
Australia. Yet on gaining its independence this island,
with its population of 2.5 million people, not only
decided to apply for membership of the Commonwealth
but also elected to have the Queen as head of state. The
country could well have become a republic within the
Commonwealth, but chose not to. The former Prime
Minister of Papua New Guinea, Michael Somare, helps to
explain something of the 'magic' about the Queen and
the Commonwealth.

*Receiving gifts from
Cook Islanders*

We could have chosen to be members of the Commonwealth and thus recognise the Queen as Head of the Commonwealth and not as head of state. But we are close to Australia and the Queen was Queen of Australia. When the time came for us to discuss the course our constitutional development should take, we went around and sought out people's views. They all said they wanted to have the Queen as head of state. . . .

When the Queen comes to my country she is accorded the normal greeting: guard of honour inspections, trooping of the colour, 21-gun salutes and so on. And there are also tribal dances and ceremonies of course. But in meeting the Queen in their traditional festivities, people see in her someone who is above tribal loyalty and tribal conflict. That's the role of the Queen.

The Royal party on Pentecost Island, 1974. They were watching a display by land divers, who launched themselves from a platform ninety feet high with a length of vine tied round their ankles to break their fall just short of the ground. Tragically, heavy rains had stretched the vines and one man was killed

CHAPTER 5

Africa

'She could quite easily be elected Queen of all the world'
Zambian Daily Mail, June 1979

'If the Commonwealth is to thrive, it has no choice but to engage the big issues of our time.'
MALCOLM FRASER *Former Australian Prime Minister*

The colonial conquest of the continent of Africa took place to all intents and purposes in the late nineteenth century. For about forty years before the outbreak of the First World War, European adventurers and traders carved up Africa between them. Dividing tribes and creating unnatural boundaries, they exploited the resources they found in abundance. Where there were few resources, as in some of the poorer desert regions, the boundaries themselves were manipulated to establish a less-than-perfect political map which put (virtually) the entire continent of Africa under the control of one European country or another: Belgium, France, Holland, Portugal, Spain, Germany. But by far the largest imperial power was Britain.

In 1920, twenty of today's independent states on the mainland continent of Africa were under British rule. Sixty years later every one of them was independent and thirteen had become members of the Commonwealth. In West Africa, there are the two oldest colonies: Gambia and Ghana (formerly the Gold Coast). These were the countries from which slaves had been shipped off to the new Americas. Later came Sierra Leone and Nigeria, now the largest and arguably richest country in Africa.

The Queen is given a traditional Nigerian welcome on her 1956 tour. Nigeria became an independent republic in 1960

The horsemen of Kaduna, Nigeria, line the route to greet the Queen

*Inspecting the
Sword of Honour in
Lagos*

East Africa was colonised later still, for its resources, and Zambia (Northern Rhodesia), Zimbabwe (Southern Rhodesia), Malawi (Nyasaland), Tanzania (Tanganyika and Zanzibar), Kenya and Uganda were all largely settled in the nineteenth century.

In southern Africa there are three tiny states in uncomfortable proximity to South Africa: Botswana (Bechuanaland) is a republic, whereas Lesotho (Basuto-land) and Swaziland have their own monarchs.

The rest are all republics, but they include some of the Commonwealth's most enthusiastic supporters and among the leaders are some of the Queen's most devoted admirers – a feeling which is unquestionably mutual. She has known and enjoyed the company of, amongst others, Dr Julius Nyerere, the former President of Tanzania; Dr Hastings Banda, the Life President of Malawi; and President Kenneth Kaunda of Zambia for many years.

In her thirty-three years as Head of the Commonwealth, the Queen's stature has increased enormously. Presidents and prime ministers of former colonies express the greatest respect for the reservoir of her knowledge and experience. Combined with a winning, warm and perceptive personality, these qualities provide the foundations for the success of the Commonwealth ideal.

The Queen is shown a blacksmith's shop in Sierra Leone, 1961

The fact that the Commonwealth prime ministers have direct access to the Queen without going through Downing Street, and the fact that during her long reign the Queen has come to know personally all Commonwealth heads of government, will always give her a great advantage over some of her British ministers where

A large gift of flow-ers from a tiny girl in Nigeria...

...and a little boy who didn't want to give up his bouquet. He was born on the same day as Prince Charles, and named Prince after him

Commonwealth affairs are concerned. It's an advantage which the Queen uses sparingly, but always to great effect.

Ghana in 1961 was an excellent example. It has been said by some that the Palace works hard at maintaining the Commonwealth connection because it affords the British monarch a status far greater than that enjoyed by other European kings or queens. That may or may not be so, but what the Queen has consistently proved is that nothing will stand in the way of her devotion to the Commonwealth.

In 1961, the Queen took a personal line in deciding to go ahead with her state visit to Ghana. Four years earlier the country had been assisted in the full transition from its existence as the Gold Coast to the sovereign state of Ghana. By 1961, however, Ghanaian internal politics were in turmoil. As seen from Whitehall, President

Kwame Nkrumah was in the process of setting up a police state. He had put some opposition leaders behind bars and there were explosions all around Accra.

In the circumstances, it was not surprising that Her Majesty's government expressed grave doubts about the wisdom of risking the Queen's safety in Ghana. But the Queen was determined to go. She felt strongly that cancelling her visit would be such a rebuff to the Ghanaians, wrapped up in their domestic problems, that they might leave the Commonwealth. She felt that, however serious the security situation in Accra, she should make the journey to show the Commonwealth flag, to allow the politicans and people of Ghana to think beyond their immediate problems and to remain in the fellowship of the Commonwealth. Ignoring Whitehall's advice, the Queen said: 'How silly I should look if I was scared to visit Ghana and then Khruschev went a few weeks later and had a good reception.'

The Ghanaian leader Kwame Nkrumah asks the Queen to dance on the 1961 tour. The Duke of Edinburgh is amused

*Ghanaian tribes-
men await the
Queen's arrival*

*With trays of fruit
on their heads,
Ghanaian women
line the Queen's
route*

The Queen's decision to go to Ghana led to an extraordinary development. The Commonwealth Secretary at the time, Duncan Sandys, agreed to go to Ghana in advance and 'try it on the dog'. So off he went to Accra and, accompanied by President Nkrumah, he drove with stately deliberation along the proposed Royal route. Not only did the two complete their drive in complete safety but, far from encountering hostility, they were greeted with wild enthusiasm.

An interesting footnote to the incident is that Nkrumah was himself delighted to have a British politician for company on a drive through the streets of Accra. His actions during the run-up to the Queen's visit had alienated large sections of his people, and it had reached the point where he had been scared even to be seen in the streets of the capital. So he too had approached the drive along the proposed Royal route with some trepidation. But when the extraordinary little procession reached the

A sun hat for the Duke of Edinburgh in Ghana, 1961

end of its journey, Ghanaians – who had at first been bemused – rushed forward in their hundreds and mobbed Nkrumah. And, of course, the Queen and her Commonwealth Secretary survived the later visit.

Four years later the Queen took another personal initiative in Commonwealth policy. It concerned Rhodesia, where Prime Minister Ian Smith was locked in a bitter dispute with Whitehall over his refusal to give his African population, which outnumbered the whites by about 25 to 1, full voting rights.

The wily Ian Smith attempted to get British public opinion on his side by trying to disguise the essentially racist nature of the dispute and by asserting that his country was not quarrelling with the Crown or with fellow Britons at home, but with the 'ludicrous' ideas of a British Labour government.

With one decisive stroke, the Queen disabused Mr Smith and his white supremacists of the idea that they clothed their actions in the colours of the Union Jack. In her own hand, she despatched a personal letter to the Rhodesian Prime Minister, making it clear that it was not possible to claim loyalty to the Crown and Commonwealth and at the same time defend white supremacy. The letter read:

> Dear Mr Smith,
> I have followed the recent discussions between
> the British government and your government
> with the closest concern, and I am very glad to
> know that Mr Wilson will be paying you a visit. I
> earnestly hope that your discussions will succeed
> in finding a solution to the current difficulties. I
> cherish memories of my own visit to Rhodesia. I
> should be glad if you would accept my good
> wishes and convey them to all my peoples in your
> country, whose welfare and happiness I have
> closely at heart.
> Yours sincerely,
> Elizabeth R.

By her use of the plural 'all my peoples', not even Mr Smith could believe that Her Majesty was only referring to the white population of the country. A fortnight later, when Smith made his unilateral declaration of independence (UDI), it was done without the benefit of the Crown's blessing or the approval of the British government.

In his book *Stitches In Time* the first ever Commonwealth Secretary-General, Arnold Smith, gives an interesting insight into how far the Queen might have gone, had she been allowed, in trying to settle the Rhodesia issue. Smith recalls:

> At my first audience after Rhodesia's UDI in 1965, I said it was a pity that Britain had never used its power to disallow discriminatory laws against the African majority, and told her I had proposed to Harold Wilson a plan for nipping UDI in the bud by sending in British paratroops and asking her to broadcast to the Rhodesian people. She did not comment directly on these points, but I had the impression that she would have willingly taken a more active role in the Rhodesian crisis, had Wilson asked her to do so.

Even so, the Queen went a great deal further than British monarchs are usually allowed to go in their involvement in foreign affairs. It is well known, for example, that the Queen's father had been eager to take a personal initiative to avert the slide to the Second World War. The King had prepared a draft of a personal letter he intended to send to Hitler but, although he tried repeatedly to persuade his government, the Prime Minister – Neville Chamberlain – and the Foreign Secretary – Lord Halifax – refused to let the King send his letter. The King, it was felt, was too important a national symbol to be allowed to involve himself in something which might fail.

Despite the Queen's concern over Rhodesia, it did not bring Ian Smith to heel. It did, however, leave him in no doubt about the attitude of the Queen of Britain and the Head of the Commonwealth, and in that respect it is seen as having been most significant.

The Rhodesian problem was to come up in the

Commonwealth context again, however, and when it did the Queen was determined to exercise her Commonwealth role to the full. In 1979, there was a new incumbent at No 10 Downing Street. Margaret Thatcher had been voted into office in May and, while on a visit to Australia some two months later, she said that for security reasons she felt that the Queen should not go to the heads of government meeting to be held later that year in Lusaka. Twenty-four hours after Mrs Thatcher had spoken in Australia, a terse announcement from Buckingham Palace said the Queen had 'every intention' of going to Zambia, after visits to Tanzania, Malawi and Botswana, and that Prince Philip and Prince Andrew would be going along with her.

Once again, as in the case of Ghana eighteen years before, there were legitimate security concerns. The declaration of UDI in Rhodesia had been followed by an attempt to get Britain to recognise a 'puppet' government led by Bishop Abel Muzorewa. Muzorewa's government was being opposed by nationalist guerrillas, some of whom were based in the Zambian capital, Lusaka, and the fighting had spread to Zambia. One morning, not very long before the Queen was due to arrive, an explosion in the Zambian capital shook the pictures off the wall in State House – the office of the Zambian President, Kenneth Kaunda. The bombing had been the work of Rhodesian Selous scouts, who had crossed the border, driven into Lusaka, planted the bomb (which was intended to kill Joshua Nkomo, one of the guerrilla leaders) and had driven out again undetected. That was the state of Zambian security.

The Commonwealth leaders were scheduled to spend their traditional informal 'weekend break' in Livingstone – an area of unrivalled beauty but hardly a safe 'retreat'. Had they gone, they might have peered across the Zambesi and found themselves looking straight down the barrels of Rhodesian guns.

There was another consideration occupying the Queen's thoughts, however, which was more important than her own safety. It would be her first visit to Zambia, and President Kaunda and his compatriots were looking

for the Royal seal of approval on their hosting of the Commonwealth heads of government meeting. It would also be the first time the Queen would be present for such a Commonwealth gathering in a Commonwealth republic. But the pressure on her not to go was unrelenting.

The newspapers took up the cry about the Queen's safety. From Salisbury, Bishop Muzorewa was quoted as saying that 'no one can guarantee' a trouble-free Commonwealth meeting. He added, rather ominously, since his were the forces crossing into Zambia to attack the guerrillas, 'I think they are taking a risk having the meeting in Zambia.' And when Joshua Nkomo was persuaded to declare a two-week ceasefire while the Queen was in Zambia, so that Muzorewa's forces would have no pretext to launch counter-raids inside Zambia, one British columnist boldly asserted: '[Nkomo] should be told to go to hell. The Queen does not need, nor does she seek, any safe conduct from [him].'

No wonder when the Queen's VC 10 touched down at Lusaka airport towards the end of July 1979 that most of

Children dancing for the Queen during a short visit to Botswana in 1979

the population of the Zambian capital turned out to greet her. For merely agreeing to come to Zambia, the Zambian *Daily Mail* went into ecstasy about the Queen's visit, and another paper reported an enthusiastic verdict from a sermon by a Zambian priest who likened her arrival in Lusaka to the 'second coming': the banner headline was 'THE SECOND COMING: QUEEN AS JESUS?'

But before all that, the Royal tour had begun in Tanzania. In Dar Es Salaam, roses were flown in from Kilimanjaro and special dishes were ordered to celebrate the arrival of the 'Great Malkia'. On the burning tarmac Ngomo dancers pounded out their enthusiastic welcome and then, at a state banquet, the Queen spoke about the freedom of the individual in oppressive regimes.

'You are almost the same age as my mother and there's no stopping you,' the Queen had once teased Malawi's Dr Hastings Banda, and her greeting there was as warm and friendly as ever. At a state banquet which was given for her, she was totally absorbed in her conversation with Dr Banda, whom she has known from her teens. The Queen ate little and probably didn't hear much of the music either, as a string orchestra struggled to come to terms with those most British of tunes – 'Berkshire Hills' and 'Hearts of Oak'.

In Botswana, which the Queen had been urged to visit by Dr David Owen when he was Foreign Secretary, the Queen was commended by Sir Seretse Khama for her 'great personal courage and commitment' in her determination to visit southern Africa. Sir Seretse Khama said she was making her visit 'at the most difficult period in the history of the area'. He was not only referring to the Rhodesian war, but to the issue which faced the Zambian Commonwealth meeting: how to settle the political impasse which had led to the fighting.

The role played by the Queen at Commonwealth meetings is something of a conundrum. She is always around at the time of the meetings, but she never attends any formal sessions and she does not declare the meeting open. But she sees all the prime ministers and heads of government individually.

These meetings are valued greatly, not only by the Queen but by the heads of government, who have come to respect her advice and her counsel. It's made all the easier because the presidents and prime ministers are never in doubt about Her Majesty's commitment to the Commonwealth, and they welcome the opportunity to talk to someone whose presence symbolises everything the Commonwealth stands for. Prime ministers say that at these meetings the Queen listens, asks questions which always indicate a thorough grasp of national or regional problems and, by putting her prestige behind the interests of the Commonwealth, she can frequently ease the way to solutions to these problems.

Before the start of Commonwealth heads of government meetings, her timetable for seeing prime ministers can frequently look like the diary of an over-ambitious world traveller:

10.00	Australia	10.40	Nigeria
10.20	Fiji	11.00	Seychelles

Before seeing a prime minister, the Queen has usually had a final briefing on the country from her private secretary. She would also have had flashed from the Admiralty the script of the 3 am BBC overseas service, and she would probably have read a digest of the world and home news from a report sent by the Central Office of Information in London. Exchanges between the Queen and Commonwealth prime ministers are never bland, and the prime ministers usually come away impressed.

In Lusaka the Queen played an important role in the deliberations of the Conference, not directly but behind the scenes. She urged Mrs Thatcher to do everything to avoid the Commonwealth breaking up over the Rhodesia issue, she talked the Nigerians into toning down their threats to leave the Commonwealth, and she encouraged the Australians and the host nation Zambia to try to find a solution to the problem. This was successful. Britain agreed to new Rhodesian elections under a new constitution.

Dr Hastings Banda introduces Her Majesty to some of his countrywomen, 1979

A tête-à-tête with Kenneth Kaunda at the time of the Lusaka heads of government meeting. Kaunda is holding his ever-present white handkerchief

The Queen made a special stopover in Nairobi in 1972 to see Jomo Kenyatta, who plucked a rose from his garden and presented it to her. She carried it for the rest of the afternoon

President Kaunda is full of praise for the Queen's role:

> It's her personality, her thoughts toward man-
> kind, which make her such a welcome contribu-
> tor to what goes on at these summits. At the
> Lusaka meeting in 1979 she played a very vital
> role. The Queen is an outstanding diplomat;
> that's how she gets things done. . . .
>
> There were criticisms about the conference
> being held in Zambia, especially from the right-
> wing members of the British press. The Queen
> took a personal decision to come. When she
> arrived, she found it a very tense situation. But,
> mainly because of her own personal involvement,
> tempers cooled. Because we all realise her com-
> mitment to the Commonwealth, we all respond to
> her messages of conciliation.

The Australian Foreign Minister at the time of the
Lusaka summit was Andrew Peacock, who visited
Tanzania after the Queen. He agrees with President
Kaunda about the atmosphere created by the Queen's
presence at Commonwealth meetings. He said he found
that Her Majesty's visit to Lusaka had induced a
mellowing feeling towards Britain at a crucial moment
before the Commonwealth deliberations actually
began.

After the meeting, the Commonwealth Secretary-
General, Sir Shridath Ramphal, was one of the many
who tried to sum up what the Queen had achieved:

> Her Majesty is among the best informed of all
> Commonwealth watchers. The Rhodesia issue
> threatened to tear the Commonwealth apart. At
> the crucial time, the Queen exercised her stabilis-
> ing influence. She was diplomatically brilliant.
> The Queen brought to Lusaka a healing touch of
> rather special significance.

The New Zealand Prime Minister, David Lange, said of
the Queen's involvement in the settlement which ended
the Rhodesian war:

The Queen does not skirt around the major political issues. She is very well aware of them and you are left in no doubt about that. She is perceptive. She puts forward a view and that is what it stays at. She'll never make a statement, she's not going to make a public speech; she'll not attend one executive session of a Commonwealth summit. But hers is the unifying presence. We, the Commonwealth leaders, do the fighting over the political issues. She does the unifying.

She has said that her role is to do just that – to promote unity, and that's what she did with such astonishing success in Lusaka.

The Queen's tour and her visit to Zambia had been a triumph. Her Majesty could hardly contain her emotion when thousands of people gathered to see her off. As her VC 10 lifted off the tarmac, she could still see President Kaunda waving his white handkerchief and, although she could not hear them by this time, the crowds were still chanting: 'Bye bye, Queenie.' To tumultuous cheers, one emotional commentator exclaimed: 'We can all tell our children that once upon a time we saw a most gracious and beautiful lady, the Queen.'

By her decision to go to Lusaka, the Queen had successfully reminded everyone of her ability to rise above the transient threats and the political tension which can beset even Commonwealth relations. Her devotion to the Commonwealth ideal – to the extraordinary grouping of different nations and cultures and races – against all the odds handsomely won the day.

A decade earlier, she had expressed her view about dissensions within the Commonwealth. 'The nations belonging to the Commonwealth,' she said, 'have in their hands a well tried framework for mutual help and co-operation. It would be short-sighted to waste this modest step towards brotherhood because we are too busy with dissensions of the moment.' Her Majesty's final verdict on the Lusaka conference was that it had again established the Commonwealth's 'uniquely effective system for bringing progress out of conflict'. Those

are her words and they are fitting because, at Lusaka in
1979, the Commonwealth stepped back from the brink.

Sighs of both relief and satisfaction were breathed
when the Lancaster House Conference that followed the
Lusaka summit finally brought Rhodesia to legal independence. The new state of Zimbabwe was born in April
1980, and immediately applied to join the Commonwealth.

The troubles of Africa seem to be the besetting problem
of most Commonwealth meetings, and the country that
has given most worry – almost to the point where the
very existence of the Commonwealth has been
threatened – has been South Africa.

Until the country's withdrawal in 1961, the policy of
apartheid had made it increasingly difficult for the
newly independent black African states to sit at the same
conference table and mix socially with South African
leaders. Then, in 1971, Edward Heath came up against
concerted Commonwealth opposition to his government's proposal to resume arms sales to South Africa. At
the end of that Conference a consensus declaration was
made that kept the Commonwealth countries together
without actually resolving their differences.

In 1985, in Nassau in the Bahamas, the problem of
South Africa once again dominated the Conference.
There were five days of often heated discussion, all of it in
private, when the British Prime Minister argued her case
against imposing sanctions on South Africa. Ranged
against her seemed to be the rest of the Commonwealth.
As the discussions continued at what should have been a
relaxed weekend of social get-togethers, there was dark
talk among the press that the Commonwealth would be
seen to be divided this time.

Until her departure for the rest of her Caribbean tour,
the Queen had kept in close touch with the debate. Each
head of government that came to see her on board
Britannia brought news and opinions, and never for one
moment was she in any doubt about the importance
of the issue. Eventually, a consensus was reached, and
the Commonwealth was once more seen to be united.

CHAPTER 6

Canada

'There is a sense of fairness about the way Commonwealth meetings are conducted. We're all treated equally, no one gets to stand at the back of the line.'
BRIAN MULRONEY *Canadian Prime Minister*

The Queen's first visit to Canada was in 1948 as a newly married princess with her husband. It is the Commonwealth country by far the most frequently visited by any member of the Royal Family, and the Queen herself has been on no less than fourteen occasions. This cosseting of Canada, the most senior and, along with the UK, arguably the most influential member of the Commonwealth, is both sensible and desirable.

After the declaration of independence of Britain's American colonies in 1776, there was serious concern in London that Canada might follow her neighbour's example. A report in 1839 by Lord Durham showed that there was serious discontent in the Canadian colonies, and Lord Durham proposed that in future the Governor of Canada should appoint ministers who had the confidence of the local assembly, and that he should accept their views on all domestic matters. By 1867 Canada had become the first of the self-governing dominions and, along with Australia, New Zealand, South Africa and Britain, was one of the founder members of the old British Commonwealth.

By the Statute of Westminster in 1931, Canada became fully independent, but it was not until 1982 that the last constitutional links with Britain were finally severed. Although Westminster's role as the ultimate power over the Canadian constitution had been purely formal for fifty years, it was strongly felt in Ottawa that it was an anomaly that should be corrected, and so in 1982 the Queen proclaimed the new constitution at an open-air ceremony on Parliament Hill in Ottawa and, in the words of Pierre Trudeau, 'Canada severed its last colonial link with Britain'. The new Canadian constitution did, however, retain the Queen as head of state.

All the Queen's horses and all the Queen's men. The Queen becomes the first reigning monarch to open Parliament in Canada, 1957

It is perhaps surprising that Canadians should have such a strong attachment to the Queen because, while many of its original settlers came from Britain, it has over the years become a 'melting-pot' society of European immigrants. For example, there are over half a million Canadians of Ukrainian descent in Alberta. Some years ago, they learned that they had something in common with Her Majesty when a University department of political science discovered that the Queen had a lineal connection with a medieval Ukrainian prince – news which was hailed with great joy by the Ukrainian community.

The population of Canada is now 25 million, but the only indigenous Canadians are the 400,000 Indians and Eskimos. With both of these ethnic minorities the Queen has a mutual bond of respect and affection. However, the second largest grouping after the 9.5 million Canadians who claim British descent are the French Canadians.

There are 6 million Canadians of French ancestry, and the country is officially bi-lingual. Canadian governments always maintain a close relationship with France, and Prime Minister Brian Mulroney recently attended a meeting in Paris that was set up to discuss the formation of a Commonwealth-type grouping of Francophone states. The idea of setting up a 'French Commonwealth' on similar lines to the British Commonwealth has been raised and debated from time to time, and the concept of 'la francophonie' – or closer relations between French-speaking peoples – was first written about in the 1880s. But it was not until the end of the 1960s that organisational plans began to be made, and the movement then started with African leaders rather than with the French.

Some forty French-speaking nations were represented at the Paris conference in 1986, including a number of Commonwealth countries: Vanuatu, Mauritius, St Lucia and Dominica, as well as Canada. *The Economist* commented that 'they [the French] will soon find, as the British have done, that – as in many family parties – the part the younger participants enjoy best is the chance to criticise Mother'.

The Queen has always been sensitive to this French connection and careful to acknowledge it whenever she visits the predominantly French-speaking provinces. In her very first visit to Canada as Queen she addressed the nation in a seven-minute live broadcast, part of which she delivered in French. During her 1964 visit she spoke in French to a 'gathering of notables' at 'her ancient

*There is a mutual
bond of affection
and respect between
the Queen and
Canada's indige-
nous peoples – the
Indians and
Eskimos.*

capital of Quebec', as she had done in 1959 when she visited the city for the first time as reigning monarch. And, mindful of the fact that Ottawa is the capital of both French and English-speaking Canadas, she called it 'la capitale de la civilisation française en Amérique'.

At the height of French nationalism in Quebec, particularly in the sixties and seventies, the role of the Crown was challenged by those who considered it no longer a valid representation of themselves. President de Gaulle fuelled the flames of separatism when, during a visit to Quebec in 1967, he shouted from the balcony of the Montreal City Hall, 'Vive le Québec libre!' The Queen herself has been heckled on occasions, to the point at which Prince Philip told French-Canadians bluntly in 1970:

> The answer to this question of the monarchy is very simple – if the people don't want it, they should change it. But let us part on amicable terms and not have a row. The monarchy exists not for its own benefit, but for that of the country. We don't come here for our health. We can think of better ways of enjoying ourselves.

Her Majesty has many happy memories of her Canadian visits, however. Her first as Queen was a visit to Ottawa in 1957 when she opened Parliament, the first reigning monarch to do so. The fashion note of the visit was not the Coronation gown which she wore to open Parliament, but the extravagant Norman Hartnell gown which she wore at a reception. This became known as the 'Maple Leaf of Canada' dress. The broad garland of maple leaves on the dress was appliquéd with crystals and emeralds among which were scattered white roses of York aglitter with crystals, diamonds and pearls.

On her second tour in 1959 the Queen spent six weeks in June and July travelling all over the country and visiting outlying districts never before seen by a reigning monarch. She opened the new St Lawrence Seaway and, sailing down it in *Britannia*, which had been specially modified for the journey, made her first television appearance. The producer remembers that she was very

Her Majesty wearing her famous 'Maple Leaf of Canada' dress at a state dinner in Ottawa

A Royal encounter at Whitehorse, once a famous centre in the days of the Yukon Gold Rush

nervous in front of the camera, and Prince Philip stepped forward with a cryptic bit of advice. 'Remind her of the weeping and gnashing of teeth,' he said. The significance of that was lost on the producer and his crew, but it did the trick. The Queen relaxed and the broadcast was a great success.

The Queen remembers that visit for another reason, however. Having welcomed the Canadian Prime Minister, John Diefenbaker, and the American President, Dwight Eisenhower, and his wife Mamie aboard *Britannia*, she took Mrs Eisenhower aside to tell her that she was expecting her third child, Prince Andrew. Later, when she stood on deck with the American President and the Canadian Prime Minister, the crowds down below shouted: 'Ike, we love the Queen.'

Her Majesty discovered on that 1959 Canadian trip that the country was 'simply too big' to be fully covered in a single tour, and since then tours have concentrated on specific areas. In 1964 she returned to Canada for the centennial celebrations in October commemorating the visits of the Fathers of Confederation to Charlottetown and Quebec City.

While she was there, there was almost a terrible accident. On returning to the *Britannia* after a state banquet ashore one evening, the Queen was just about to board when she noticed a perceptible movement from the gangplank. 'It moved,' she said, arching her eyebrows, 'I'm not going up there.' For a while nothing happened. But then, with the entire Royal retinue watching, *Britannia's* gangplank parted from its platform with a frightful noise. Nothing much was said, though there were a few embarrassed faces as *Britannia's* crew set to work to repair the damage. When the gangway had been firmly secured to its platform, Prince Philip's voice was heard cutting through the icy atmosphere with the quip, 'We'd better get up quickly before anything else gives way.'

In 1967 the Queen had the opportunity to cover a great deal more of Canada by involving other members of the Royal Family on the tour. She wanted as many of them as possible to be associated with Canada's celebrations,

commemorating the hundredth anniversary of the Confederation, and it was also the year of Expo 67. This was how the Royal schedule looked:

14 May – 9 June   Princess Alexandra and the Hon. Angus Ogilvy – Ontario, the four Western Provinces, the Yukon and North-West Territories.

29 June – 5 July   The Queen and the Duke of Edinburgh – Ottawa and Expo 67, Montreal.

10–22 July   Queen Elizabeth, the Queen Mother – the four Atlantic Provinces.

22–23 July   The Duke of Edinburgh – Winnipeg.

Late in the afternoon of 29 June, the Queen and Prince Philip arrived in Ottawa. Thousands of people lined the route as the Royal couple were driven through the city to Government House. In the next few days the Queen attended religious and civic ceremonies to mark Canada's hundredth birthday, and at the Canadian Pavilion at the Expo 67 exhibition she took an unscheduled ride on the mini-rail.

On the Queen Mother's twelve-day tour of the four Atlantic Provinces she used the Royal yacht as a mobile residence. This is the way the Queen likes to see *Britannia* used, and it is a popular symbol of the Royal presence abroad. After one visit to Canada, the yacht was crammed on her way home with hundreds of gifts. Their variety was extraordinary – from a chunk of iron ore to a mink coat fit to be worn by a Queen. There was also a painting of an industrial scene, a pair of snow shoes, a condiments jar, a sackful of spears and an umbrella.

Today *Britannia* is decorated with scores of mementoes from Commonwealth tours. There's a curious-looking mallet used by Tongan women at work, a *porai*, which is used by Tongan men as a fighting club, and a shark carved in driftwood from Fiji. As a reminder of her first Commonwealth tour in the SS *Gothic*, Her Majesty has retained a settee, an armchair and some silver from the old ship. And when the Gambians gave the Queen a baby crocodile in a pierced silver biscuit tin, it found a place in the bath of Her Majesty's private secretary.

The Queen returned to Canada in 1970 with Prince

Cutting the cake at Canada's centenary celebrations, 1967 – Prince Philip moves forward to help as the knife gets stuck

Charles and Princess Anne for the centenary of the North-West Territories and the province of Manitoba, and again in 1971 for the centennial celebrations of the province of British Columbia.

In 1973 she was determined to be in Ottawa for the Commonwealth heads of government meeting. She has said of these meetings:

> I welcome the chance of hearing about the problems which Commonwealth countries face, when individual ministers from the Commonwealth come to London, and also on such special occasions as prime ministers' meetings. At moments like this, I have the benefit not only of getting to know some of my prime ministers better, but of welcoming the new nations of the Commonwealth.

The 1973 visit was planned with meticulous care. Even when she is as far away as Regina or Calgary, the Queen must receive her state papers, her 'red boxes', which are taken to her by Queen's messenger. Only the Queen or her private secretary may unlock these secure boxes. The logistics on the 1973 Canadian tour were so complicated that a special appointment was made, that of the Queen's Canadian secretary; he went personally more than twenty times to all the places the Queen intended to visit, just to ensure that all the arrangements were sound.

The Queen was delighted with the results of all this hard work, and enjoyed being in Canada at the time of the Commonwealth meeting. She said afterwards that it had been 'a family occasion' which reminded her of 'the importance of human relationships in world affairs and how membership of the Commonwealth has a subtle influence on the relationship between its leaders'.

The host of the meeting was the Canadian Prime Minister, Pierre Trudeau. When he had first taken office in 1968, Trudeau was somewhat lukewarm about the benefits of Commonwealth membership. He attended his first Commonwealth meeting in London in 1969 and openly admitted that he was sceptical about the value of the association. He had something of a reputation as a

The 1970 visit to the North-West Territories was a family affair. The Queen and Princess Anne are warmly wrapped against the cold in anoraks they had been given

On board Britannia, *going through the red boxes that follow Her Majesty wherever she goes*

'swinger' at the time, which was augmented after a famous incident during Harold Wilson's reception at Lancaster House when he found the magnificent curving banister irresistible. With a cry of 'Olé!' he jumped on it and slid down into view of the journalists below.

However, he played a very significant role at the next heads of government meeting at Singapore, when it was generally recognised that his pragmatic intervention helped to solve the thorny problem of British arms sales to South Africa. He was an excellent chairman of the 1973 Ottawa heads of government meeting and it was by this time clear that his belief in the Commonwealth was genuine. He said:

> We find value in gathering together periodically
> because we believe there is merit in candid
> talk. . . . There is no other forum available for this
> purpose for political decision-makers from all
> parts of the world. . . . There is no graduate
> school to prepare heads of government for their
> tasks, no sabbatical refresher courses, no evening

Yet another speech during the exhaustive 1977 Jubilee tour . . . this time it's Ottawa

seminars or summer schools. Unless we talk to
one another about our experiences and techniques of governing, we are not able to broaden
our own horizons.

Although he has now retired from active politics, Pierre
Trudeau will be remembered as one of the Commonwealth's most radical spokesmen and one of its undoubted leaders.

Other Canadian prime ministers have also played
their part in keeping the Commonwealth together. In
many cases Canadian influence has been used to help the
Commonwealth to extricate itself from British attitudes
and policies which were likely to damage it. For
example, in 1949 Canada urged that India should be
allowed to remain as a member of the Commonwealth in
its new status as a republic. In 1961 John Diefenbaker
was a key figure at the heads of government meeting
when South Africa withdrew from the Commonwealth,
and in 1969 Trudeau's predecessor Lester Pearson
persuaded African leaders to give British Prime Minister
Harold Wilson more time to settle the Rhodesian
problem.

The present Prime Minister of Canada, Brian Mulroney, went to his first Commonwealth heads of government meeting in Nassau in 1985, accompanied by his
pretty young wife Mila and their six-week-old baby son.
He saw very little of either as he was propelled into the
debate on South Africa. During the weekend retreat at
Lyford Cay it was he and Rajiv Gandhi, another
newcomer, who emerged as the key figures in trying to
sway Mrs Thatcher in the sanctions discussions. It was
said by certain members of the press that it wasn't for
their negotiating skill that Mulroney and Gandhi were
put up against the British Prime Minister, but because of
their persuasive charm and the effect this had on Mrs
Thatcher.

In many ways, Canada epitomises the ideals of the
Commonwealth itself. It has never been totally self-
preoccupied, despite some isolationist lapses, and it has

always shown vision. The peaceful way in which it gained its independence from Britain set a pattern for millions of other colonial peoples to follow. And, because it has never considered itself a great power, Canada realised from its earliest times that it could never hope to be entirely self-sufficient – either politically, strategically, economically or, for that matter, culturally.

Canada has always been anxious to demonstrate its independence from its giant neighbour, the United States, on whom it must rely so heavily, and has found an international role in its dedication to the Commonwealth. This realisation has fostered in Canadian statesmen a profound belief in the instruments for collective decision-making and consultation. While older countries have sometimes suffered from encrustations of tradition, Canada has always been progressive, and the Canadian spirit was more than a match for the developing Commonwealth association. Both have benefited from the other. The evolution of the Commonwealth broadened Canada's thinking and its horizons. Its first diplomatic missions were opened in India and Pakistan on the Asian sub-continent, and its first mission in Africa was set up in another new Commonwealth country, Ghana. In return for the acquisition of this broader international profile, Canadians took the lead in development assistance for less well-endowed Commonwealth countries.

This is why the Queen likes and admires Canadians so much. She has publicly praised their industrial development and their enlightened lead in international relations.

Canada has responded to the admiration and trust placed in it, not only by the Queen, but by other members of the Commonwealth, with its material contributions. The country's contribution to Commonwealth finances is second only to that of Britain. Out of the £5.5 million budget of the Commonwealth Secretariat, Britain pays 30 per cent and Canada 17 per cent, whereas many of the very small members contribute less than 1 per cent. Canada also contributes considerably in terms of expertise towards the Commonwealth Fund for Technical

Prince Charles appears unsure about the attractions of this embroidered handbag at a Women's Institute bazaar

The Queen inspects a traditional embroidered quilt

Co-operation, as well as giving generous bi-lateral aid to several Commonwealth countries.

A knowledge and affection for Canada extends to the next Royal generation, and Prince Andrew spent some time at school in Ontario at Lakefield College. During the Queen's 1982 visit to Canada he was on active service with the Royal Navy, and Her Majesty was provided with a special 'hot line' which followed her wherever she went, so that she could keep in touch with 10 Downing Street and the situation in the Falklands.

Some Canadians felt that the Queen looked unusually glum during that tour. And word even leaked to one enquiring Toronto journalist, apparently via a member of Her Majesty's household, that in her sterner moods the Queen had earned the nickname 'Miss Piggy'. The Queen heard about it because the journalist used the story, but the incident caused no enquiries among her staff. Her Majesty found it amusing.

What the Queen remembers most about her Canadian trips is the way in which Canada's ethnic diversity resembles the make-up of the Commonwealth. Reflecting on her Canadian trips, she saw in them a lesson on the strength of her Commonwealth family.

In Canada, we met some of the older inhabitants – Indians – whose ancestors were there for generations before the Europeans came. And further north still live the Eskimos, some of the most interesting people we met during our travels. . . . They too belong to the Commonwealth family, this remarkable collection of friendly people of so many races.

CHAPTER 7

The West Indies

'The Caribbean is a miniature version of the
Commonwealth.'
HER MAJESTY THE QUEEN on 1985 West Indies tour

'She is our Queen. She wears the crown for England and
she wears it for Barbados too.' BARBADIAN WOMAN, 1985

The Commonwealth Caribbean countries stretch in a
graceful curve from the southern tip of Florida in North
America to the continental shelf of South America. In
between are the French colonies, former Dutch dependencies and a few tiny American islands, making
together a necklace of tropical pearls encircling the
Caribbean Sea.

The Caribbean has always had a special place in the
hearts of the Royal Family. When Princess Margaret had
her six-week honeymoon in the West Indies in 1960, she
asked that the privacy of the event be respected. That is
not a concept that immediately appeals to the ebullient
West Indians, however, and they responded in the only
way they know. The Princess and her husband were met
on their 'private' honeymoon by a flotilla of small boats,
helicopters and steel-bands, calypso singers and colourful native dancers – and by photographers galore. The
Princess, who had always had a soft spot for the area,
took it all in her stride and, far from being offended,
made on the islands her winter holiday home.

The Queen loves the islands of the Caribbean for their
diversity. She has said that they look to her like a
'miniature version of the Commonwealth'.

To the north are the 700 or so tiny islets and rocky outposts of the Bahamas, so near to Miami that they look every inch an extension of the North American continent, broken up by blamelessly blue waters and sparkling white beaches. Much further south is Barbados, whose unquestioned English outlook is underscored by the frequent repetition of the story that, during the Second World War, the island sent a telegram to Buckingham Palace and to Winston Churchill pledging loyalty and support in the struggle and adding: 'Go ahead Britain, Barbados is behind you.'

Crowds cheer the Queen on her visit to a straw market in Nassau, 1966

Alone among its Caribbean neighbours, Barbados never changed hands, remaining British throughout the great eighteenth-century European scramble for overseas possessions. Today the names of its towns and parishes and counties are reminiscent of Dorset and Hampshire and Wiltshire.

Barbadians waiting to see the Queen drive past on her visit to the island in 1985 showed that their affection for Britain and for her monarch seems to have survived the centuries intact. 'She is a charming lady,' remarked one woman, 'and she doesn't seem to be getting old.' From another the comment was: 'She is a lovely lady. God put her there and she does good for all the poor people of this island.' 'She is still number one,' said another lady, 'and Britain is still the mother country of all the Caribbean islands.'

When the Queen came to the throne, the islands of the Caribbean had already set out on the steady road to peaceful political self-determination. Full internal self-government in the late nineteen-fifties was followed by an attempt to link all the Commonwealth territories in a West Indian Federation. The attempt failed, and four years later the march to independence began. Jamaica was followed by Trinidad and Tobago and Guyana, and the movement quickly spread, like a raging forest fire, to the other islands. Today Guyana, Trinidad and Tobago and Dominica are republics within the Commonwealth, while the Queen is head of state in the other islands – including Barbados, Antigua, St Vincent, St Kitts and Grenada.

Jamaica was the second stop on Her Majesty's great Commonwealth tour in the autumn of 1953, the year of her Coronation at Westminster Abbey. She came back to the Caribbean in 1966 when she made a full tour of the islands, and she went to Jamaica again in April 1975 during the meeting in Kingston of the Commonwealth heads of government. Two years later the Bahamas, Antigua, the British Virgin islands and Barbados were included in her Jubilee tour. She was back in the Caribbean in 1983 and in 1985 returned to the region during the Nassau Commonwealth Conference to visit

*Another day,
another island – a
warm welcome from
schoolchildren on
St Kitts*

*A local woman
shows her affection
for the Royal Family
on the Queen's 1966
tour*

the Bahamas, Belize, St Kitts Nevis, Antigua, Dominica, St Lucia, St Vincent and the Grenadines, Barbados, Grenada and Trinidad and Tobago.

In every island she went to on the 1985 tour, the Queen preached the same message – the value of the Commonwealth. She reminded the people of St Lucia, at a rally in the Mindoo Phillip Park, of the Commonwealth's 'real contribution toward the prevention of disagreements and violence'. She congratulated the people of St Vincent on their independence and on their decision to become 'a full and independent member of the Commonwealth, with all the rights, responsibilities and privileges of this remarkable organisation that binds together the English-speaking peoples'.

In Barbados, she spoke at a rally in the stadium opened by the Prince of Wales fifteen years before, and she reminded her audience of the emphasis she had placed in her Commonwealth Day message on 'the importance of young people seizing the opportunities provided by modern communications to increase their knowledge of other nations of the Commonwealth'.

In Antigua she praised the new spirit of the Commonwealth, and said that as its Head she was impressed by its ability to 'stimulate economic progress, growth and national development'.

She also conferred the OBE on the West Indian cricketer Andy Roberts at an investiture, and in her speech praised that other great West Indian player Viv Richards. It struck an extremely popular chord since on an earlier visit to the Caribbean the Queen had performed the ceremony which made Gary Sobers Sir Garfield.

The part of Her Majesty's tour that most interested the American press was her visit to Grenada. One member of the Royal household, referring to this in advance of the event, said, 'We're going to re-take Grenada.' It was an obvious reference to what the Queen in her speech opening the new Grenadian Parliament called the 'momentous events' of 1983. On 25 October of that year American forces, apparently at the request of the Organisation of Eastern Caribbean States, invaded

Grenada after the murder of the leader of the People's Revolutionary Government, Prime Minister Maurice Bishop.

Grenada is an independent Commonwealth country and the invasion raised a number of constitutional questions about the role of the Queen's representative, her Governor-General, Sir Paul Scoon. The Queen had not been informed beforehand about the invasion, and Mrs Thatcher's government in Britain was therefore bound to raise questions about the American intervention. The involvement of other Commonwealth Caribbean states – most notably Barbados and Dominica – confused the issue somewhat, but in general the incident cast serious questions about the meaning of the 'Commonwealth link'.

After heated general debate, the conclusion seems to have been reached that the Governor-General of Grenada had the right, as laid down by the Grenadian constitution, to exercise the powers of the Crown in seeking outside assistance to restore civil order in his country after the chaos and killings which followed the murder of its Prime Minister.

Her Majesty's view now is that Grenada has emerged from the experience with 'tremendous credit'. She made it clear that she did not believe that the island's Commonwealth connections had in any way been impaired by the experience. And in 1985 she stressed the positive outcome of the recent troubles.

> As your Queen, I want to take this opportunity of congratulating the people of Grenada on the way you carried through the recent Parliamentary elections which underlined your commitment to democracy. It has been a notable achievement and the world has watched with admiration. More remains to be done and your friends in the Commonwealth . . . will help you in the process of reconstruction.

The first stop on the Queen's tour had been Belize – a country on the east coast of Central America whose neighbours are Mexico and Guatemala – and, as she said,

Her Majesty stops to chat to Antiguans on her 1985 tour

The Queen knighting Gary Sobers, 1975

one of her 'eighteen realms' she had not visited before. The people of what used to be called British Honduras became independent in 1981 and opted to retain Her Majesty as head of state. The main language of Belize is English, but Spanish, Creole, Carib and Maya are also spoken there, and in many ways it seems an unlikely Commonwealth country – not that you'd think it to listen to the speech made by the Prime Minister, Manuel Esquivel, in the country's National Assembly.

> Our people affirm their loyalty and warm affec-
> tion to your Majesty's person and to your family
> and their respect for the institutions they have
> inherited. . . . The sovereign, united, democratic
> state of Belize reaffirms its commitment to the
> system of government that vests executive
> authority in Your Majesty, Elizabeth the Second,
> by the Grace of God, Queen of Belize. . . .
> May this House, furnished with your Majesty's
> gifts, be always worthy of Your Majesty's favour,
> as we strive to create for our people a free,
> prosperous and secure future, with opportunity,
> equality and justice available to all Your
> Majesty's subjects. The people of Belize welcome
> you into our hearts and our homes; our land is your
> land, our homes are your homes.

This speech of welcome to Her Majesty, with its almost medieval expressions of loyalty, is a striking example of the affection and respect which the Queen commands in all her Commonwealth countries.

After Belize, the Queen went to the Bahamas, where her Commonwealth prime ministers and heads of government were meeting.

If Belize, with its Central American geography and landscape, looks an unlikely member of a Common-wealth which evolved out of British influence, the Bahamas stretch the very concept of that Common-wealth. The people of the islands do claim descent from early English colonists who came to the area after fleeing North America during the American Revolution. But that was two hundred years ago.

Today the islands are more in step with the frenetic tempo of New York or Miami than with the reflective quiet of English life. Because Nassau is only half an hour's flying time from southern Florida, 2.5 million Americans make the Bahamas their holiday playground every year. They don't require passports, and when they reach Nassau they can stay in American-style motels, eat hamburgers and clam chowder and drink American beer – all at American prices. American radio and television programmes swamp the air-waves, and the Bahamas dollar and its more illustrious American counterpart are interchangeable.

In Nassau, the Queen saw all the heads of government in private audience before the meeting, and hosted a dinner in their honour aboard *Britannia*.

Considerable press comment arose out of the fact that the heads of government were all late for dinner. They had been due aboard at quarter to eight, but by half past less than half of them had arrived. The Queen was photographed on the deck of *Britannia* looking out to shore anxiously and drumming her fingers, a gesture generally perceived as a sign of right Royal impatience. But when the prime ministers eventually turned up with their explanations the Queen, far from being annoyed, was highly amused.

The reason for their lateness turned out to be that they had decided to travel from the Conference Hall to *Britannia* by sea instead of the more conventional route by road. Their journey had evidently taken them some distance out to sea because several of them looked distinctly ill on their arrival. The Queen herself is no stranger to that experience and is usually sympathetic to fellow sufferers, but that evening in Nassau she could hardly stop herself enjoying a joke at their expense.

'Why did you go all round that way?' she enquired. The prime ministers had to admit the delicate reason that they had been trying to avoid a quayside demonstration against the Prime Minister of the Bahamas. There had been several already on the trip, with posters which welcomed the Queen but deplored alleged corruption in the country.

On being told that the intention had been to avoid the demonstrators, the Queen exclaimed: 'But whatever for? We've all seen those demonstrations and the banners. They say "The Chief's a thief"!' With that, the prime ministers' embarrassment at being less than punctual dissolved into light-hearted mirth.

The Queen was enjoying it all too. She took personal charge before dinner of the placing arrangements for the 'family photo' of her Commonwealth heads and herself. Her press secretary was busily trying to show the heads to their appointed places in the line-up, but she kept saying: 'Please get out of the way, Michael!' with a mischievous smile, insisting on doing it all and thoroughly enjoying herself. Needless to say, they all did precisely as they were told.

When the heads of government had been properly placed for the Commonwealth family picture, Her Majesty then took charge of the photographers. 'Have you got enough?' she asked, knowing that they had but that they would never admit it. Without waiting for a reply, the Queen got up and swept her prime ministers in to dinner.

Banquets on *Britannia* are elaborate affairs. Former Prime Minister Pierre Trudeau says that the first thing one notices is how absolutely clean and perfectly arranged everything is. 'Parts of other ships look oily and grimy,' says Trudeau, 'but on *Britannia* the Queen and her guests can eat off the floor if they so desire.'

They don't. Guests sit with their Royal hosts at a magnificent table which can comfortably seat fifty-six, and which takes at least three hours to set – with each knife and fork and spoon in its precisely correct position. It is said that the Keeper of the Royal Apartments is so careful about these placings and about where each glass should go in relation to the others that a ruler is used to ensure the precision.

The menus are always in French, and guests are allowed to take them home as souvenirs – although some guests try to make off with the silver napkin-holders as well. But it's always embarrassing to be asked to give them back. 'We do ask for them back,' says one member

Nassau decked out for the Queen's arrival for the Commonwealth heads of government meeting in 1985

The population of Nassau demonstrate their dissatisfaction with their Prime Minister in front of the Queen

of the Royal household. 'We couldn't afford to lose the number guests will take.' The Queen's cypher is on each of the five glasses at each setting: one for water (Malvern bottled water is the Queen's favourite), two for wine, one for champagne and the fifth for port.

The menus are all planned before *Britannia* leaves her home port, and the kitchens on board are large and palatial enough to cope with a banquet seven days a week. Wines come out with the ship from London and, wherever possible, the Queen likes to serve the wine of the country she is visiting. In non-wine-growing Commonwealth countries like the Bahamas, French wine and French champagne is served.

There was not the slightest hint of alarm from *Britannia*'s chef at the late arrival of the heads of government for the banquet in Nassau, but one prime minister commented that the meal had been served with the greatest efficiency and with the most decorous speed.

One reason for this is that banquets are often just one part of an evening's programme. There's usually music on board during dinner, but occasionally the band of the Royal Marines also plays on the quayside after dinner or after a reception. Time must be allowed for that after the brandy and cigars.

When the Marines are playing for the Beating the Retreat, which guests watch from *Britannia*, the tunes are always inescapably British – wherever Her Majesty may be visiting. In the Bahamas after one reception for Commonwealth heads of government officials, the Royal Marines played 'Hearts of Oak', 'Men of Harlech', 'John Peel', 'Danny Boy' – and even 'Rule Britannia' and 'Land of Hope and Glory'.

This is an extraordinary testimony to the way in which the Commonwealth family is happy in its relationship with Britain. It's a mature relationship now – based not so much on the past, but forward-looking and confident. That is what the Queen's influence has enabled the Commonwealth to become, and this is how the Queen herself sees the modern Commonwealth. In her 1984 Christmas message she described its birth as 'one of the more encouraging developments since the war'. And she

added, 'Like a child it has grown, matured and strengthened, until today the vision of its future is one of
increasing understanding and co-operation between its
members.' The majority of the quarrels of the past have
been subjugated to thoughts about what it can do in the
contemporary world and in the future.

The Queen sees this as important too, and one of the
ways in which she attempts to demonstrate that
commitment to the Commonwealth's future is in her
interest in young people. The West Indies tour of 1985
was a splendid example of this. The Queen attended
youth rallies in almost every Caribbean island she
visited. Many of these were held in the broiling sun with
temperatures in the high 80s. But given the chance to
speak from the comfort of a shaded platform canopy, or
to drive among the ranks of young people, the Queen
always chose the latter. Repeatedly in her speeches she
has said to the young people of the Commonwealth:

> You are the future. What you do now and what
> you learn now will determine how best you can
> serve the Commonwealth in years to come. So
> think now of learning about other Common-
> wealth countries. Think about travelling to those
> countries. Think how best you can serve the
> family of nations.

Her own knowledge of what goes on in Commonwealth
countries is wide-ranging and formidable. In Barbados
the Queen had to do the round of business enterprises,
one of them a cement works in which she could not have
been terribly interested. But she listened intently to the
complex industrial and chemical processes involved in
cement-making and will no doubt demonstrate on some
later occasion her grasp of the subject to some hapless
prime minister or minister of works.

In the Bahamas, her knowledge of the world of
gambling took some heads of government by surprise.
She asked a group of Commonwealth leaders at a
reception on board *Britannia* whether they knew why it
was that so many hundreds of thousands of Americans
came to the Bahamas every year to play in the casinos. (It

was not an entirely inappropriate subject since the Commonwealth Conference hotel in Nassau had shut down one of the more popular casinos for the duration of the meeting.)

The clutch of prime ministers had not given the matter much thought and were unable to say. The Queen delightedly answered her own question by informing them that there were only three states in America where gambling in casinos was legal, and since there were so many gamblers the Bahamas, being so close, were assured of business. 'It took us all very much by surprise,' said the Fijian Prime Minister, 'we have all come to respect Her Majesty's knowledge of many things, but we didn't think she was such an expert on American gambling laws. We were impressed.'

All in all, it had been a highly successful tour of the West Indies, made more so by the fact that the Queen and Prince Philip could go to the various stopping-off points on board *Britannia*. Indeed, the tour wouldn't have been possible without her. The yacht's company of 21 officers and 260 men dedicate their lives to making the Royal couple as comfortable and as happy as possible, and one striking feature of the life on board is the quiet. Orders are not shouted but given by signal when the Queen and the Duke take their walks around the decks, and everything is done with little fuss and a minimum of noise.

During the 1985 Commonwealth meeting, *Britannia* moored in Nassau alongside the cruise ships from Miami. The Royal yacht is a travelling palace, and discharges many of the functions of a palace. Over a period of three days the Queen met forty-six Commonwealth heads of government, entertaining them to dinner on one evening and their officials on another.

For the last four days of her visit she never left the ship; her daily exercise was taken on the deck of *Britannia*, usually on the side away from the gaze of American tourists. The official visit to the Bahamas ended when *Britannia* slipped her moorings at Nassau to the rhythmic beat of the Royal Bahamian Police band

Britannia *under
fireworks*

The main conference room where the heads of government debated in Nassau, 1985

and sailed off south into the Caribbean night. Before resuming the tour the Royal party had four days at sea to relax from the official programme.

Two months after her return from the Caribbean the *Britannia* set sail again, a 12,000-mile voyage ahead of her before meeting the Queen in New Zealand towards the end of February 1986. But her smooth passage was interrupted before she cleared the Red Sea. A civil war in Aden was making life intolerable for foreign nationals, and the British Government had advised all Britons to leave; the only way out was by sea. As the British families made their way to the beach under heavy gunfire, they saw to their amazement *Britannia* moored off-shore. It was the Queen's own yacht that had come to their rescue.

Under the command of Rear-Admiral John Garnier, *Britannia* carried them to Djibouti across the Gulf of Aden before returning for more refugees. Over a period of six days, she made six journeys to pick up a total of 1082 refugees from fifty different countries – including 79 Britons, 109 Chinese, 25 East Germans and 2 Argentinians. Every part of the ship with the single exception of the Queen's own bedroom was used to make the refugees comfortable.

The Queen was 'delighted' that *Britannia* had been of such valiant service.

CHAPTER EIGHT

The Commonwealth Games

'I am glad to say that contacts at all levels between Commonwealth countries continue to grow. . . . Among the people who attract greatest attention are visiting sportsmen and athletes.' HER MAJESTY THE QUEEN

The Commonwealth Games have always had a distinctive image. In the violent, recriminatory cut-and-thrust of international sport, they have managed to maintain an enviable image as 'the friendly Games'. Perhaps it could be no other way, not only because of the spirit which pervades Commonwealth contacts at all levels, but because the interest of the Queen and other members of the Royal Family in the Games perpetuates and nourishes that spirit.

The Queen has also perceived an important practical aspect of the Games, however. Wider international events like the Olympics had for a long time proved to be beyond the prowess of many African countries, and certainly gave no opportunity for athletes from some of the smaller Commonwealth countries like St Vincent, Fiji or Tuvalu. The Commonwealth Games not only provided that opportunity, but helped athletes from smaller countries to achieve such a standard that they were soon pressing their claims in the larger international arena. Today's internationally known runners, riders and weightlifters of Kenya, Ghana, Nigeria, Trinidad and Jamaica first became household names in the Commonwealth. In the 1970s the Queen, commenting on the success of Kenya's Kip Keino, expressed the hope that 'many more sportsmen from Africa will take part in competitions to establish new contacts between Africa and the rest of the world'. Today that is no longer a hope, but a reality.

The historical progenitor of the modern Commonwealth Games was an 'Inter Empire Sports Meeting' which was held for the first time in London in 1911 after the coronation of George V. The competing countries were the United Kingdom and the dominions of Canada, South Africa and Australia, New Zealand and Tasmania. There were only nine events but, even so, it was a great success. Canada was declared the overall winner and the team was presented with the Lonsdale Cup, an impressive silver trophy 2 foot 6 inches tall and weighing 340 ounces. (With the subsequent approval of the Earl of Lonsdale and of Canada, the trophy was melted down in 1934 and several cups were made to a 1712 Queen Anne design. The replicas were distributed amongst Commonwealth countries, the principal cup being held by the Commonwealth Games Federation.)

The success of the 1911 Sports Meeting led to a stream of suggestions about how it might be made a regular event, and in 1928 the manager of the Canadian Track and Field Team, Bobby Robinson, was authorised by the civic leaders in Hamilton to present a proposal to hold the first 'British Empire Games' in that city. Robinson met with other representatives of Empire countries in Holland, but too many problems were raised. Undaunted, he returned to London in January 1930 and, after weeks of negotiations in which the Canadians made generous offers of free lodging and travel grants for competitors, it was agreed that the first 'British Empire Games' should take place in Hamilton from 16 to 23 August 1930.

The manner in which the Empire Games would differ from other international events like the Olympics had, even in those early days, been carefully considered. The statement after the London meeting read:

> It will be designed on the Olympic model, both in
> general construction and its stern definition of
> the Amateur. But the games will be very differ-

ent, free from both the excessive stimulus and the babel of the international stadium. They should be merrier, less stern and will substitute the stimulus of novel adventure for the pressure of international rivalry.

It is a remarkable fact that, nearly sixty years later, the Commonwealth Games still hold to that statement of intent. 'Merrier and less stern' – that has been the code by which successive Commonwealth Games have been staged.

The 1930 Hamilton Games were opened by the Governor-General of Canada on behalf of King George V, and messages were read out from both the King and the

The spirit of the Commonwealth Games – Australian swimmer Lorraine Crapp with members of the Ghana team in Cardiff

Prince of Wales. This set the pattern for other Empire and Commonwealth competitions, and today no Commonwealth Games is without some Royal presence. The Queen is patron of the Commonwealth Games Federation, and the Duke of Edinburgh has been its president since 1955. He has been present at all the subsequent Games and, with the exception of Edmonton in 1978, has participated in the opening ceremonies and read the Queen's message. The Queen also makes every effort to be present for some part of the Games; she opened the 1978 Games and will be in Edinburgh in 1986 for the closing ceremony. She was also there in 1970 to close the Games, as well as in Christchurch in 1974 and Brisbane in 1982. Prince Charles, Princess Anne, Prince Andrew and Prince Edward have all attended the Games at some time.

Four hundred competitors took part in those first Games in Hamilton. They came from Australia, England, Bermuda, Newfoundland, New Zealand, Northern Ireland, Scotland, South Africa and Wales. The generous spirit which is such a feature of the modern Commonwealth Games was evident even in those early days. In the third heat of the 100 yards, a New Zealand sprinter was quite properly disqualified after two false starts. However, the crowd protested so noisily about this that the organisers had to allow him back before the race could continue. A far cry from the Olympics!

It was agreed to hold the Games every four years and, in August 1934, 50,000 spectators watched the opening ceremonies of the second British Empire Games at the White City Stadium in London. The number of countries taking part had now increased with the addition of Hong Kong, India, Jamaica, Rhodesia and Trinidad. Four years later, in Sydney, Fiji and Ceylon took part, and when the Games resumed after the Second World War Malaya, Singapore and Nigeria made their debut in Auckland in 1950.

Ceylon won its first gold medal there, the winner of the marathon was attacked by a dog three miles from the finish, and a hurdler had to be content with a bronze medal because he lost a button on his shorts and only 'the pumping action of his legs kept him from embarrassment'. These highlights aside, though, the Games had clearly begun to fulfil their function, emphasising the 'stimulus of novel adventure' as against 'the pressure of international rivalry'.

If it hadn't before, the world began to take notice in 1954, when the Games were held in Vancouver, Canada. It was the year in which Roger Bannister won the historic sub-four-minute mile, and he repeated this at Vancouver in a classic encounter with the Australian John Landy. Bannister's time was 3 minutes 58.8 seconds, against Landy's 3 minutes 59.6.

The Vancouver Games will also be remembered for a memorable display of courage by Jim Peters, the 35-year-old captain of the England track team. Stumbling into the stadium at the end of the marathon, Peters had only a lap to go to win the gold medal. But, crippled by exhaustion, he fell down eleven times as, staggering and crawling, he attempted to reach the tape. He tried in vain for more than fifteen minutes, before falling into the arms of the English masseur. Spectators who watched this heart-rending display of raw courage called it 'the most heroic display of running ever seen'.

The Games ceased to be called Empire Games in 1954, and became known as the British Empire and Commonwealth Games.

The 1958 Games in Cardiff broke ten world records. Murray Halberg, the New Zealander with the withered arm, won the three-mile event; the great Herb Elliot of Australia won the 880-yards event and the mile race; there were gold medal performances from Keith Gardner of Jamaica, Milka Singh of India and England's Geoff Elliott; and in the swimming Dawn Fraser and Lorraine Crapp were the Australian stars. The Cardiff Games also offered a tantalising glimpse of the future. Nigeria and Uganda appeared among the medal winners, and were soon to be joined by Ghana, Kenya, Malawi, Tanzania and Zambia. The Asian Commonwealth nations, India and Pakistan, also did well, winning four gold medals between them.

A feature of the opening ceremonies of subsequent

The British Empire and Commonwealth Games, 1958. The Commonwealth has given to the world the concept of 'friendly' international rivalry

Games (except those of 1962) was introduced in Cardiff. At Buckingham Palace the Queen handed over her 'Games message' to a relay of runners – Roger Bannister, Chris Chataway and Peter Driver – all gold medallists for England in the 1954 Games. The message was enclosed in a specially designed silver-gilt baton, and a series of runners carried it to Cardiff. This ceremonial baton was later placed on permanent exhibition, but new batons have been designed for subsequent Games. The message is read at the opening ceremony, usually by the Duke of Edinburgh. For the Commonwealth Games in Edmonton in 1978 the Queen handed over her address in London, but opened the Games herself.

The closing ceremony of the 1958 Games was distinguished by a tape-recorded message from Her Majesty, who told the enthusiastic crowd that she had chosen the

*Competitors at the
1958 Games*

occasion 'to create my son Charles Prince of Wales
today'. The intermingling of athletes and officials after
the Queen's message in a mass gesture of common
friendship brought the Games to a memorable end.

There had, however, been one important political
issue at these Games, which in many respects reflected
the changing face of the Commonwealth. It was not
entirely accidental that at the Games which marked a

Cardiff, 1958. Herb Elliot, a twenty-year-old Australian clerk, receives the gold medal for winning the one-mile race

significant increase in the number of black African nations competing, there should have been protest demonstrations in Cardiff and London about South Africa's team being selected 'on the basis of colour rather than ability'. The Queen never said anything publicly about the issue, though her views must have been easy to guess given her oft-stated dedication to a Commonwealth representing 'an equal partnership of nations and races' among people 'of many creeds and colours'.

Grayling of South Africa catches an upper-cut to the chin from Kawere of Uganda during the boxing events at Cardiff. These were the last games in which South Africa competed

It was clear that South Africa had no part to play in an increasingly multi-racial association, and Cardiff was the last Games the country competed in. It came as little surprise when she withdrew from the Commonwealth three years later. South Africa's domestic policies were diametrically opposed to the noble ideals of the emerging Commonwealth, a fact which had been noted as far back as 1934. South Africa had been awarded the honour of hosting that year's Games, but at a meeting during the Los Angeles Olympic Games in 1932 it was decided that South Africa's attitude to black athletes could hardly be held up as an advertisement for these 'friendly games'.

Today the question of South Africa's participation in any international sporting event has become one of the dominant political issues of our time. The Commonwealth took a significant lead in dealing with the issue by issuing its 'statement on apartheid in sport', otherwise known as the Gleneagles Agreement, hammered out during a conference in London at the time of the Queen's Silver Jubilee in 1977. The statement says:

> The member countries of the Commonwealth, embracing peoples of diverse races, colours, languages and faiths . . . recognise racial prejudice and discrimination as a dangerous sickness and an unmitigated evil and are pledged to use all their efforts to foster human dignity everywhere.

The Gleneagles Agreement commits member countries to do everything they can to combat the evil of apartheid by 'withholding any form of support for, and by taking every practical step to discourage, contact or competition by their nations with sporting organisations, teams or sportsmen from South Africa or from any other country where sports are organised on the basis of race, colour or ethnic origin'. And the Agreement welcomed the belief that there were 'unlikely to be future sporting contacts of any significance between Commonwealth countries or their nationals and South Africa while the country continues to pursue the detestable policy of apartheid'.

In the 1962 Commonwealth Games in Australia, the host country dominated the swimming events. Dawn Fraser won two individual titles, though England's Anita Lonsborough won three gold medals and two went to fifteen-year-old Linda Ludgrove. On the track, there were superb examples of emerging African power when

Roche of Australia and Songok of Kenya clear the last hurdle in the 440-yards men's hurdle in Perth, 1962

Seraphino Antao of Kenya won the men's 100- and 220-yards events.

But the Perth Games will also be remembered for its moving closing ceremony, which the Duke of Edinburgh stayed to watch long after he had been scheduled to leave. A Welsh boxer, Rocky James, led the 700-voice choir through Australia's 'Waltzing Matilda', after which the athletes marched out arm-in-arm, totally engulfing the Duke of Edinburgh's open car.

One editorial in an Australian paper the following day summed it up simply:

The Perth Games have undoubtedly achieved their primary objective – that of promoting friendship among the multiplicity of races, colours and creeds who make up the Commonwealth. The scenes at the closing ceremony with athletes from a score of different countries all holding hands and singing and laughing around the Duke of Edinburgh is a good pattern for the whole world.

With that, the Queen would no doubt wholeheartedly agree, believing as she does that the Commonwealth is 'one of the true unifying bonds in this torn world'.

In 1966 Jamaica, at the time the smallest independent and the only predominantly black country ever to stage the Games, played host to the teams of thirty-four countries. For the first time, Prince Charles and Princess Anne accompanied the Duke of Edinburgh to the Games, and in her Christmas Broadcast that year the Queen made a special mention of the fact: 'My two elder children came back from the Commonwealth Games in Jamaica enchanted with the adventure, the kindness of the people, and the opportunity to meet so many athletes from every part of the Commonwealth.'

The Games had, by 1966, dropped the word 'Empire', and were now known as the British Commonwealth Games. In the mile race, the first six finishers all broke the four-minute mile. Kip Keino, one of the Queen's favourites, won both the mile and the three-mile events, and the unknown Naftali Temu took the six-mile race. Roger Gibbon of Trinidad won a cycling gold medal, and the Isle of Man obtained its first gold medal ever.

In the 1970 Commonwealth Games in Edinburgh, Kip Keino won the 5000-metres event, and his compatriots Charles Asati and Robert Ouku won four medals between them. African middle-distance runners had burst on to the world stage, and a total of eight gold medals went to Commonwealth African nations.

An Australian schoolgirl, Raelene Boyle, picked up a gold medal in one of the relay events; a seventeen-year-old Jamaican, Marilyn Neufville, completed the 400-metre event in the world record time of 51 seconds; the Australians claimed twelve gold medals in the fourteen swimming events; and Canada, England and Malaysia took the honours in the badminton competition. Hong Kong won its first ever gold medal at the Games in the fours event, and India and Pakistan won five gold medals each in the wrestling.

At the conclusion of the Edinburgh Games, the 1400 competitors and 400 officials from 42 Commonwealth

The legendary Kip Keino of Kenya leading the field in his favourite 1500-metre event in Edinburgh, 1970

The first ever 1500-metre race for women at the 1970 Commonwealth Games. Two more paces and New Zealand's Sylvia Potts would have beaten Rita Ridley of England, but she collapsed from exhaustion inches from the finishing tape

countries invaded the competition track and entirely surrounded the jeep carrying Her Majesty the Queen on her lap of honour. There had never been a greater or more spontaneous expression of Commonwealth joy. The Queen had entertained the athletes on a bitterly cold day at a large garden party in the grounds of Holyrood House before the competition actually began. But the Games ended on a brilliant sunny afternoon, and the competitors of various colours and nationalities joined hands in a memorable parade of singing and dancing around the athletic track. No other international sporting event can boast of such an atmosphere.

The 1974 Games in Christchurch, New Zealand, maintained the tradition of relaying the Queen's opening message by baton. It was read by the Duke of Edinburgh, who was there on several days to see Tanzania and St Vincent win their first gold medals and to see the phenomenal Michael Wenden of Australia win a personal total of nine gold medals, the highest ever won by a single athlete in the history of the Games.

Another piece of history was made at the Christchurch Games – it was decided that from now on the word 'British' would be omitted from future Games. So Canada, which had hosted the first 'British Empire Games' in 1930 and the fifth 'Empire and Commonwealth Games' in 1954, became the first country to do so under their new simple title of the 'Commonwealth Games'.

The eleventh Commonwealth Games in Edmonton in 1978 were attended by a record-breaking 1500 athletes from forty-six Commonwealth countries. The Queen was visiting Canada at the time, and she was present to open the Games with her two youngest children, Prince Andrew and Prince Edward, in attendance. The Duke of Edinburgh stayed on to close the Games. Canada was the most successful winning team with 45 gold medals, and their Graham Smith was the undoubted star. He won 6 gold medals in the swimming events, a feat surpassed only by Mark Spitz in the 1972 Olympics.

In 1982 the Games were held in Australia for the third time, in Brisbane, and were opened by the Duke of

Edinburgh to a background of 60,000 flag-waving spectators. Once again, competitors from all over the Commonwealth took part, including two from the Falkland Islands – in the full-bore rifle shooting event – only weeks after the end of the Falklands War. Fittingly, the Australians won the most gold medals, 39, with Britain second with 38 and Canada third with 26. The Queen was present towards the end of the Games to present medals and attend the spectacular closing ceremony which included carnival floats, parachutists, a Chinese dragon and a gigantic Waltzing Matilda. The Royal car, flanked by athletes, made two laps of the arena to the strains of 'Auld Lang Syne'.

When the Commonwealth Games Federation met to decide a venue for the 1986 Games, their task was not as difficult as it had been in previous years. Edinburgh quickly emerged as the only possible candidate – awarding the Games to one city twice was an unorthodox but logical step forward.

It is no longer possible today, with so many world economies locked in recession, for the massively expensive building programmes that are necessary to stage the Games to be undertaken by a different country every four years. Commonwealth cities which already have the required facilities will find themselves increasingly called upon to be hosts for the Games. Edinburgh's Meadowbank Stadium, Royal Commonwealth Pool and Pollock Halls residential village were designed to accommodate far more than a once-in-a-lifetime festival of sport. And Scotland welcomes the opportunity to demonstrate the direction in which the Games must progress into the next century.

For the first time, the team numbers will exceed 2500. For the first time the Games will be substantially financed by commercial interests, an essential initiative if standards are to be maintained. This is very different from those early days in the 1930s when host countries bore the financial burdens of inviting and accommodating Commonwealth teams. And 1986 will see a number of sporting firsts: the first-ever women's

Her Majesty at the
award ceremony,
Christchurch, 1974

Colourful ceremonies at the Commonwealth Games in Brisbane, 1982

marathon, the first-ever women's 10,000 metres, the first women's bowling event, the first synchronised swimming event and the first boxing superheavyweight division.

After the 1982 Games in Brisbane, the Queen explained why she feels they are so important.

Any of you who attended or watched the events at the Commonwealth Games at Brisbane cannot have failed to notice the unique atmosphere of friendly rivalry and the generous applause for all the competitors. In a world more concerned with argument, disagreement and violence, the Games stand out as a demonstration of the better side of human nature and of the great value of the Commonwealth as an association of free and independent nations.

CHAPTER NINE

The Commonwealth in action

'The Queen has been able to use her long personal
connection with Commonwealth heads of government, and
her personal knowledge, to follow the traditional injunction
to warn, to consult, to advise and to encourage.'
JAMES CALLAGHAN *Former British Prime Minister*

When, on her coming of age, the Queen made her famous
broadcast dedicating her life, 'whether it be long or
short', to the service of the Commonwealth, it may have
occurred to some that such declarations were out of
fashion. As one historian put it: 'The words of Princess
Elizabeth today sound charmingly dated, like Peter Pan
appealing to the audience to shout that they believe in
fairies in order to save the life of Tinkerbell. But the
sincerity of the Queen's belief in the Commonwealth is
no fairy story. It persists.'

It persisted in 1964 when, as the Commonwealth was
desperately trying to make itself into something of a
more recognisable and businesslike body by setting up a
Commonwealth Secretariat, the Queen promptly offered
one of her palaces as its headquarters. Marlborough
House, in Pall Mall, was built by Christopher Wren in the
early eighteenth century for the great Duke of Marlborough, John Churchill, and his wife Sarah. It's a palace
of modest splendour and had been the main distraction
of Louis Laguerre, a godson of Louis XIV, who was
responsible for the gory scenes of French and English
soldiers slaughtering each other which now run around
the main hall and up the staircases.

It was the last home of Queen Mary, and she died there

*Marlborough
House, the home of
the Commonwealth
Secretariat*

in February 1953. Today it is a bustling office block in which 400 staff from 32 different countries handle the day-to-day running of the Commonwealth Secretariat.

The Commonwealth Secretary-General is Sir Shridath Ramphal from Guyana. Seldom called anything other than Sonny – except by his staff who refer to him as 'SG' – he has run the Secretariat with charm and good humour since 1975, and is now in his third five-year term of office. He occupies a room on the second floor that in times past served as a Royal nursery. Of his two deputies, Nigerian Chief Emeka Anyaoku has been with the Secretariat for nineteen years and occupies a beautiful corner room on the first floor which was once Queen Mary's bedroom. His principal responsibility is for the political policy of

*Commonwealth
Secretary-General
Shridath Ramphal
on the grand stair-
case at Marl-
borough House*

the Secretariat. The other deputy is a former senior British diplomat, Sir Peter Marshall, who is in charge of economic matters.

Other executives of the Secretariat also have office accommodation that would be the envy of anyone. The Director for the Commonwealth Fund for Technical Co-operation, Robert McLaren, enjoys Queen Mary's private sitting-room with its beautiful view across the gardens to the Mall.

The Edward VII panelled library is now occupied by the Director of International Affairs. Not all the books in the library are what they seem at first glance; one wall is only painted as though it is bookshelves full of books. To continue the joke the 'books' in the painted bookshelves all have pun titles such as *My Nine Lives* by A. Cat. Once inside with the door closed it is difficult to find your way out but the 'book' painted over the keyhole is entitled *Tricks upon Travellers*.

The main salon is now the magnificent Conference Room, and the Green Drawing-Room with the beautiful portrait of Queen Alexandra is used as a reception room. But perhaps the most magnificent of all is the Blenheim Salon, hung with Flemish tapestries brought back by the Duke from his great campaign. Sadly, the Commonwealth Secretariat must leave these elegant offices soon, while the old building undergoes major and necessary refurbishment.

Not only did the Secretariat benefit in a material way from the generosity of the Queen in allowing the use of one of her palaces, but this action reinforced once more the Queen's dedicated support for the Commonwealth and came at a crucial juncture in its development.

The point is made forcibly by Tanzania's Julius Nyerere, until his retirement in 1985 the longest-serving leader of a Commonwealth independent state. He says:

> The establishment of the Commonwealth Secretariat in 1965 emphasised the equality of all members, and gave final discouragement to the lingering sentiment that one member had a right to some predominance over the others. It has

enabled the Commonwealth to develop along independent lines in accordance with the interests
of all members.

For most of that the Commonwealth can thank the
Queen.

Arnold Smith, the first Commonwealth Secretary-
General, recalls that Whitehall officials needed some
Royal prodding before they accepted the Commonwealth Secretary-General's role and his position as the
Queen saw it. Attending a Palace reception for the
Diplomatic Corps in 1965, Smith and his wife found
themselves placed at the end of the line of chargés
d'affaires – in other words, right at the bottom in
protocol terms. When Prince Philip noticed this, no
doubt fully aware of Whitehall's perception of the new
Secretariat, he immediately demanded an explanation.
The result was that the following week a protocol expert
was sent to Marlborough House to inform Arnold Smith
that a new place had been found for him in the
diplomatic rankings; he would in future be put before the
line of ambassadors.

The Queen encouraged the new Secretary-General to
call on her whenever he felt the need. In his very first
weeks in office, the entire Royal Family seemed anxious
to make sure he felt welcome. He was invited to small
lunches or dinners with the Queen's secretary, the Lord
Chamberlain, the Queen Mother and the Duke of
Gloucester. There were also private lunches and dinners
with the Queen herself, and four or five times a year –
before an important trip to a Commonwealth country or
an important Commonwealth meeting – the Secretary-
General would see the Queen to brief her or to pass on to
her key papers documenting Commonwealth affairs.

That development was not generally welcomed in
Whitehall, because it meant that the chief Commonwealth officer had a route to Her Majesty which did not
go via Downing Street. But after some time, British
foreign secretaries and prime ministers grew to accept
the new convention. It was another demonstration of the
Queen's devotion to the Commonwealth, and it was quite
beyond the ability of anyone to do anything about it.

The Green Drawing-Room, where guests gather for receptions

At a Commonwealth Day reception at Marlborough House, Commonwealth MPs are presented to Her Majesty

Commonwealth leaders repay the Queen's devotion amply. For example, at the Commonwealth heads of government meeting in 1975, Kenneth Kaunda let it be known that he was proposing his country, Zambia, as the host for the 1977 summit, and that he would invite the Queen to make her first visit to the republic. There was a problem, however. The Queen had asked the British Prime Minister, Harold Wilson, to invite all the Commonwealth heads to meet in London in mid-1977 on the occasion of the Silver Jubilee of her accession to the throne. Prime Minister Wilson was keen not to be seen to oppose Kaunda by putting in a counter-bid to hold the meeting in London. But when the Commonwealth Secretary-General spoke to Kaunda privately about the matter, the Zambian President quickly deferred to Her Majesty's wishes. To coincide with the celebrations to mark the Silver Jubilee of the Head of the Commonwealth, the prime ministers and presidents came to London in 1977 – and the next summit was held in Zambia in 1979.

At a thanksgiving service on the day before the meeting began, there was graphic and colourful evidence of what makes the modern Commonwealth the multi-national, multi-cultural wonder that it is. The Callaghans and the Frasers sat beside King Moshoeshoe of Lesotho, the Kaundas, Archbishop Makarios of Cyprus and Dr Hastings Banda of Malawi. It was as the Queen had wanted it – a fitting symbol for her Silver Jubilee year. She called it 'a thanksgiving for all the good things for which our Commonwealth stands – the comradeship and co-operation it inspires and the friendship and tolerance it encourages'.

One cannot, however, ignore the fact that, at the time, Commonwealth tolerance had been stretched to the limit by Uganda's self-styled General Idi Amin. Since 1971 this Commonwealth leader had presided over a murderous and brutal regime and was fast acquiring an unenviable reputation as an idiosyncratic despot.

But with the Queen's Silver Jubilee and a Commonwealth heads of government meeting due to take place in

London, the unpredictable Amin made it plain that he wanted to attend. The House of Commons and some African countries took the view that he should be banned from entering Britain. But the government was reluctant to do that directly and passed a message through a third party that he would not be welcome. Even so, Amin announced that he was proposing to attend, and even went to the extraordinary length of demanding a plane to fly him to Heathrow. David Owen remembers that at a Mansion House dinner one evening Merlyn Rees, the then Home Secretary, came up to him and whispered, 'I've just heard a flash that Amin's plane is over Dublin and about to land.' Luckily for the British government, for the Commonwealth and for the Queen, it was a false rumour. Amin the dictator never arrived.

Some Commonwealth leaders had been concerned about the choice of London for the heads of government meeting, not because they feared any longer Britain's imperial hegemony, but because they were worried that the Queen's Jubilee celebrations might impose undue etiquette on their meeting and inhibit its customary frank exchanges. That did not happen, however. And the occasion of the Queen's Silver Jubilee provided an opportunity for the Commonwealth's leaders to reflect on its history.

At the first heads of government meeting of the Queen's reign, there were only nine prime ministers, most of them from the old dominions. In London in 1977, there were no fewer than thirty-five. What had once been an imperial cabinet had undergone a sea change and was now a non-structured association of equals, encompassing a network of ties at government and non-governmental levels in virtually every domain, and facilitating an impressive movement of goods, services, ideas and people in a remarkably non-coercive framework. In a very real sense, the Queen's Silver Jubilee was a triumphant celebration of that Commonwealth transformation.

In February of that year, the Queen and the Duke of Edinburgh had set off on a seven-week Jubilee tour. It was, in the Queen's opinion, the best possible way to mark this momentous occasion in her reign. If it was a special time for her and for her family, she wanted to share it with the peoples of her Commonwealth.

From the first stop on the tour, Western Samoa, Her Majesty's highest expectations were fulfilled. She and Prince Philip were met by the largest crowds ever. She was given traditional greetings in Samoa, she was the most honoured guest at the most elaborate banquet in Tonga, floral tributes to her reign met her everywhere she went in Fiji, and even the fiercest tribes in Papua New Guinea tipped their spears to perform a welcome dance to 'the most beautiful Queen in all the world'. In New Zealand and Australia, hundreds of thousands of people took over the streets of Sydney and Auckland to applaud the Queen's decision to share her Jubilee year with them. There had never been anything quite like it. No monarch had ever had a greater show of approbation from her people.

On her return to England, she went to Westminster to hear and to reply to loyal addresses from the Commons and the Lords. Then, after the Silver Jubilee celebrations at the Commonwealth meeting in London, she made a trip to Wales and Northern Ireland.

By October, the Queen was beginning her Silver Jubilee tour of Canada and the Caribbean. The crowds in Canada have never been surpassed, and wherever she went in the West Indies entire islands stopped work so that everyone had the chance to see her.

However, 1977 had not been in other terms a particularly auspicious year for the Commonwealth. There had been more massacres in Uganda, and the country's Anglican Archbishop had been killed while in detention. As the Queen was making her Jubilee tours of the United Kingdom, an army takeover in the former Commonwealth country of Pakistan deposed Mr Bhutto, and in South Africa the black leader Steve Biko had been killed, and the country was tottering on the brink of mass civil unrest.

And yet there was the shining magnificence of the Queen's Jubilee year. In making the decision to travel so widely during her special year, Her Majesty was again keeping faith with the Commonwealth, with her family of peoples in the United Kingdom and beyond. In a deeply cynical world her continuing belief in the Commonwealth is its greatest asset. She has never expressed this more movingly than in the early years of her reign, when she said in 1954:

> When it is night, and the wind and the rain beat upon the window, the family is most conscious of the warmth and peacefulness that surround the pleasant fireside. So our Commonwealth hearth becomes more precious than ever before in the contrast between its homely security and the storm which sometimes seems to be brewing outside, in the darkness of uncertainty and doubt that envelops the whole world.

When political differences seem to pose a threat to the continued existence of the Commonwealth, that existence is already assured through the vast array of assistance projects which are a story of Commonwealth success.

One of the greatest of those success stories is in the field of functional co-operation. The Commonwealth Fund for Technical Co-operation was established in the early 1970s to provide a level of technical assistance to poorer Commonwealth countries. But it is not simply another aid agency handing out charity from the rich to the poor nations. Its emphasis is on mutual co-operation and assistance, and so the distinction between donor and recipient is blurred.

There are at present more than 250 technical co-operation schemes set up around the Commonwealth, where technicians are brought from one country to lend their expertise to another member country. One of these technicians is Mr K. P. Shrivastava, an expert in soil erosion and irrigation who has worked for many years in the parched lands of his native India. He came to the tiny Caribbean island of Antigua in 1983 for three years, and one of his tasks was to design and construct a hillside catchment area for the collection and re-use of water. Such an experiment was badly needed as the dry climate of Antigua is well suited to the production of vegetable crops, but low rainfall is a problem especially during the harsh dry season. On the other hand, during the rainy season excessive water causes 'run-off' and soil erosion. Mr Shrivastava's experiment has been most successful, and he has also taught farmers irrigation techniques and trained women in water management for their home gardens.

Today Commonwealth organisations are involved in other issues of worldwide importance. In the area of 'women and development', for example, it aims to assist in setting the agenda for the participation of women in all aspects of national life, and a department for human rights has recently been set up in the Secretariat. These matters are clearly of interest to a far wider range of countries than those of the Commonwealth alone, and are an indication of the stature of the contemporary Commonwealth – an organisation marching with the times.

Working parties have been set up to look into matters ranging from economic development to terrorism and illicit drug-trafficking. There are Commonwealth organisations dealing with science, telecommunications, youth exchange, medical assistance, legal assistance, ecology and Commonwealth broadcasting. There are recognisable developments in the arts, and a number of official and non-official organisations promote scientific and technological co-operation. It's all a far, far cry from the Empire out of which it grew.

The biennial meeting of heads of government is of course the showpiece of the Commonwealth. After a week or so of discussion and rhetoric, declarations and accords are issued on matters of wide international moment; but it is also an excellent talking-shop for exchanging views on more mundane matters.

A feature of the meetings is what has become known as

*The 1969 Common-
wealth heads of
government meeting
at Marlborough
House*

the weekend retreat. Commonwealth heads of government, without their advisors, spend two days away from
the Conference centre in personal discussions, talking
frankly and privately. There is nothing quite like it in any
other international forum, and the Queen is known to
believe it is one of the greatest strengths of the
Commonwealth. In 1973, the leaders went off to the
bracing Canadian resort of Mount Tremblant. Two years
later the weekend retreat was an idyllic bungalow hotel
on Jamaica's stunningly beautiful west coast, and in
1977 they enjoyed the golfing seclusion of Gleneagles in
Scotland.

For the younger members of the Commonwealth this provides an opportunity to pick up tips from their older colleagues, and the informality of these occasions means that no one needs to feel a loss of face when asking advice of more experienced members.

Miss Eugenia Charles, the Prime Minister of Dominica, says: 'We belong to the United Nations, but it is too vast . . . it's good to belong to something smaller . . . which has a lot of reasons for thinking alike, for having the same motives and the same perspective.' Sir Kamisese Mara, Prime Minister of Fiji, agrees. 'Where else in the world do you have this club? It is the only group of people who speak the same language, have the same experience. Prime ministers do not go to university to learn to be prime minister; this is the best university anyone can attend as a prime minister.'

And Arnold Smith gives a graphic illustration of the richness of Commonwealth contacts. In Jamaica in 1975, he says, on the day Saigon fell, he found himself sitting around a table with Indira Gandhi, Lee Kuan Yew, Tun Razak, Harold Wilson, Gough Whitlam, Pierre Trudeau and Julius Nyerere. What material for a graduate seminar in international politics!

But valuable as these opportunities are for the heads of government, it could be said that of even more value are the meetings held by the 200 or so non-government organisations. Meeting whenever and wherever they can, they range from the Commonwealth Parliamentary Association to the Girl Guides. Doctors, vets, lawyers, engineers and nurses face similar problems wherever they are, and a Nigerian might, for example, be able to help a Tongan. Journalists also have problems, and in some Commonwealth countries the press might be considered less free than elsewhere. Sympathetic encouragement and a few useful tips can send a journalist back home strengthened in the knowledge that he has friends.

The Queen herself takes every opportunity to encourage these exchanges in her speeches and by meeting the people involved whenever she can. For example, a group of Commonwealth academics met in London early in

1985. They had a full programme which included lectures, dinners and visits to universities. But suddenly a surprise item appeared on the agenda. The Director of the Commonwealth Foundation, who was organising the visit, let it be known to the Palace that the academics were in Britain, and to everyone's delight the Queen invited them to Buckingham Palace.

The Commonwealth Foundation was set up in 1966 to promote professional co-operation within the Commonwealth. Although its budget, provided by governments, is small, it does provide for a number of short-term fellowships every year to allow professionals to undertake approved research in other parts of the Commonwealth. A nutritionist from Fiji, for example, was recently given £8000 to investigate the nutritional value of the traditional foods of the South Pacific. And in the Caribbean the Foundation is involved in a distance teaching project: students in small islands like St Lucia and Antigua are linked by satellite in two-way communication with their teacher at the University of the West Indies in Jamaica.

Two other key features are the Commonwealth Institute and the Royal Commonwealth Society in London. The Commonwealth Institute is housed in a magnificent building on the edge of London's Holland Park, opened by the Queen in 1962. Its purpose has from the outset been to foster a greater knowledge of the Commonwealth and a better understanding of its importance and worth. A great deal of material from Commonwealth countries was incorporated into the fabric of the building. Most of the timber, glass, metal, furnishings and other embellishments were gifts, many from individual governments and some from industry and commerce throughout the Commonwealth.

Although Britain continues to bear the main financial responsibility for the Institute, all Commonwealth governments provide for their own individual permanent exhibitions on display, and some contribute to other services. Over 400,000 people visit the Institute each year, not only to see the permanent exhibition of the 'Commonwealth under one roof', but also to enjoy

The Queen leaving Westminster Abbey after a Commonwealth Day multi-faith service

the concerts and colourful displays of Commonwealth culture that are an on-going feature of the Institute, an example of which was the Indian Ocean Music Village where Tanzanian students performed their national dances in the unfamiliar setting of a London park.

Perhaps the largest and most ambitious exhibition at the Commonwealth Institute in recent years was 'The Human Story'. This exhibition traced the development of our ancestors through the 35-million-year history of the human species. It was opened by the Queen, who was shown around the exhibits by the anthropologist Richard Leakey, the director of the National Museum of Kenya.

The Royal Commonwealth Society – set up by Royal Charter in 1882 as the Royal Colonial Society, later becoming the Royal Empire Society – has moved with the times despite its outward appearance of a London gentlemen's club. Once the home base for colonial civil servants on leave, its visitors now come from all over the modern Commonwealth. During the busy summer months Australian students with rucksacks mingle in the foyer with African businessmen. It is an impressive building, built in 1936 to the design of Sir Herbert Baker, one of Britain's best known architects of the time. Its elegant public rooms are panelled with woods from all over the Commonwealth. The Canada Room restaurant is panelled in Canadian yellow birch and the New Zealand Bar in rimu.

Perhaps the finest feature of the building, however, is its library, to which students come from all over the Commonwealth to use the most comprehensive collection of Commonwealth literature to be found anywhere in the world.

An annual event for which the Commonwealth is indebted to the Queen is a multi-faith 'observance' which takes place in Westminster Abbey on Commonwealth Day, the second Monday in March.

In its first years the ceremony caused great controversy in Anglican circles and was only saved by the

Queen's active diplomatic support. After the multi-faith service in St Martin-in-the-Fields in June 1966, there were loud protests in certain sections of the Church of England that a service in a Christian Church had included as its principal participants a bishop and some 'heathens'. The Queen and Prince Philip had attended the service, but that did not prevent the protests going to the Archbishop of Canterbury and even as far as the Church Synod. It appeared that many in the Church's hierarchy and in the lay congregation were opposed to a multi-faith service.

For some years thereafter the service was moved to the Guildhall. It might well have remained there but, on the Queen's initiative, from 1972 the services were held in Westminster Abbey. Her Majesty was able to do that because the Abbey does not come formally under the authority of the Bishop of London, or for that matter even under the Archbishop of Canterbury. Together with the chapels at Marlborough House and St James's Palace, Westminster Abbey is termed a 'Royal Peculiar' and comes directly under the Queen's aegis as Head of the Church of England.

The Commonwealth multi-faith service is now fully established as a popular annual event, its Royal patronage unquestioned. Religious leaders move impressively down the centre aisle, followed by young people carrying the flags of all the Commonwealth nations. A fanfare of trumpets is sounded, and four affirmations are interwoven with readings from Commonwealth high commissioners, which necessarily reflect the rich religious diversity of the Commonwealth. Prayers are said in Sanskrit, Arabic and Punjabi, and in the Pidgin language of Papua New Guinea.

The Queen's example and her dedication have encouraged other members of the Royal Family to support the Commonwealth. Princess Anne certainly does so today, and as far back as 1970 Prince Charles gave a memorable address at the Albert Hall, challenging British companies to release their young graduates for a year or two so that they could be of service to people in less developed Commonwealth countries.

The Prince told his audience of some 5000 members of

the Institute of Directors that he had gained some of his education in Australia. 'It's the country where I became a man,' the Prince said, and he related such experiences as the time he spent sleeping in a hut in New Guinea 'occupied by man-eating spiders and acid-squirting caterpillars'. He urged more travel by young people in Britain to Commonwealth countries and he chided British Airways for not offering cheap fares to enable more to do it.

At the suggestion of the Secretariat, Prince Charles has also spent time at Marlborough House seeing for himself how the Commonwealth headquarters functions, and he is deeply involved with many Commonwealth associations.

Prince Philip has championed a Commonwealth Awards scheme for young people, and for more than a quarter of a century he has sustained people's enthusiasm for the Duke of Edinburgh's Commonwealth Study Conference on Problems of Industrial Society. He has accompanied the Queen on many Commonwealth tours, as have Prince Andrew and Prince Edward, and the Queen Mother has toured several Commonwealth countries – most notably Canada, where she toured four large Canadian provinces in 1967, Canada's centennial year.

During Britain's negotiations to join the Common Market, the Queen never expressed any views on the subject. As an internationalist, she must have welcomed this broadening of Britain's involvement with her close neighbours. But she saw no inconsistency between membership of the European Community and continued co-operation with the Commonwealth. She said it would be unthinkable if Britain were to turn its back on her overseas links with other English-speaking peoples.

More publicly, broadcasting to the Commonwealth in 1972, the Queen said: 'Britain is about to join her neighbours in the European Community, and you may well ask how this will affect the Commonwealth. The new links with Europe will not replace those with the Commonwealth. They cannot alter our historical and

personal attachments with kinsmen and friends over-seas.' And there was this emphatic sentence: 'Old friends will NOT be lost. Britain will take her Commonwealth links into Europe with her.'

The Queen at home with her Beefeaters in Britain, the founding member of the Commonwealth

The Queen's advocacy of the value of the Commonwealth has not always been popular in Britain, however. The most dramatic illustration of this came after the Queen's Christmas broadcast in 1983. In the months before this, she had seen extreme poverty in India and in Bangladesh. Citing the fact that India had, despite its 700 million people, managed to become one of the leading industrial nations in the world, the Queen went on to assert that 'the greatest problem in the world today remains the gap between the rich and the poor countries'. She added, 'We shall not begin to close this gap until we hear less about nationalism and more about interdependence. One of the main aims of the Commonwealth is to make an effective contribution towards redressing the economic balance between nations.'

For some newspapers and politicians this was too much. To inflame passions even further in the televised version of the speech, the Queen had appeared in conversation about development issues with Mrs Indira Gandhi. 'You're out of order, Ma'am,' screamed one headline. And Mr Enoch Powell, cleverly disguising his anti-Commonwealth position, accused Government ministers of being responsible for the controversial ideas expressed in the speech.

The reply from Buckingham Palace was magisterial in its rebuke. One can only believe it came from the Queen herself. 'The Christmas broadcast is a *personal* message from the Queen to *her* Commonwealth. The Queen has all her people at heart, irrespective of race, creed or colour.' This did not end the constitutional argument about who advises the Queen when she speaks about Commonwealth affairs, but it put an abrupt end to the controversy over the 1983 Christmas broadcast.

The Queen continues to speak about poorer Commonwealth countries and the need for the richer North to help the developing South. She has gone on record as saying: 'I believe that in God's time all the peoples of our Commonwealth, working side by side, will attain prosperity.'

CHAPTER TEN

The future of the Commonwealth

'There's not all that much friendship in the world and friendship is valuable. It's the one thing that matters ... the Commonwealth is a collection of friends, and friends don't break up if they can help it.'
LORD HOME *Former British Prime Minister*

It is easy to be critical or rude about the Commonwealth. It can summon no mighty armies to support its cause; it can win no wars. It has no constitution, no foreign policy, no explicit principles which reflect its values. At times, defining the Commonwealth is difficult for political pragmatists, and indeed some people tend to regard it as something of a mirage or – to use the imagery of Alice in Wonderland – a Cheshire Cat which has vanished bit by bit leaving nothing but an ephemeral grin. Sceptics say it's toothless, invertebrate, amorphous.

The Queen talks about it as an organisation in which the members share 'a special relationship' and, still searching for that elusive definition, she adds that in the ideal of the Commonwealth 'we have been entrusted with something very special ... a potent force for good and one of the true unifying bonds in this torn world'.

That makes it an easy target for critics. Among the many criticisms of Her Majesty's 1983 Christmas broadcast, one newspaper described the Commonwealth as 'a silly, pretentious international grouping of no significance'. The same article went on to say: 'It represents neither any interest nor any cause. It embraces liberal democracies and corrupt dictatorships. It is without influence or power.'

However, as former Secretary-General Arnold Smith once said, despite the fact that the Commonwealth is difficult to define and has few hard principles, it has over the years acquired a number of useful habits. And today they are as useful to the world order as the more explicit policies or grandiose statements of world powers.

The Commonwealth is, and operates as, a voluntary association of those states which have experienced some form of British rule and who wish to continue to work together to further their individual and collective interests. It does not aim to coerce its members; it shares a feeling of closeness and fraternity; its meetings are informal and frank, and they take place in a spirit of co-operation where Commonwealth interest is always deemed to be more important than the pursuit of self-interest.

It cannot command, but does win loyalty – although that may not be exclusive loyalty. But its greatest virtue is its diversity. In its political and functional forums, the Commonwealth can try out ideas. It can test policies and it can embrace a network of countries around the world in doing this, a network unlike any other in the world.

In the political field, it helps the world to negotiate, although unable itself to negotiate. At its two-yearly meetings, it can discuss world issues in an atmosphere unmatched in any other world forum. It aims never to fight in public or to issue inflammatory dissenting communiqués, but strives for consensus. This is what is known as the 'Commonwealth spirit'. While the rest of the world shouts about the need for a North/South bridge-building dialogue, the Commonwealth is the organisation best placed actually to do something about it. And it does.

Arnold Smith argues that the modern Commonwealth is of the greatest relevance to the international problems faced today by nations everywhere. The interdependence of all the countries in the world has been emphasised by jets and satellites and, in the global village of the twentieth century, the Commonwealth underscores the value of neighbourhood co-operation. He has said:

The growing scale of neighbourhood is simply a fact, for good or evil. The moral and political challenge of turning it into a neighbourly community remains – and the stakes involved in success or failure increase with the growing technical power to help or destroy. The Commonwealth is one of the world's most useful instruments to help its members meet that challenge.

To build a global community we must stretch the horizons of knowledge, understanding and goodwill, and develop habits of consultation and co-operation that will transcend the limits of race, religion, or economic level. That is precisely what the Commonwealth is about.

And that is the Commonwealth the Queen is proud to head. She sees it as an organisation whose members, fired by the Commonwealth ideal, strive to help their fellow members; a body in which there are disagreements, but one in which these are settled not by shouting or by armed intervention, but by friendly discussions and persuasion. A Commonwealth made up of people of all races, creeds, religious beliefs, taking in a quarter of all the people in the world – people who belong to a family, and quite a remarkable and talented family at that.

The Queen herself has been an essential factor in the development of the Commonwealth. The role of Head of the Commonwealth was born out of a happy compromise whereby India abandoned allegiance to the Crown, while accepting the monarch as the 'symbol' of the British Commonwealth in order that it could remain within the association. At that time nobody really knew what the role of the Head would be, and George VI did not live long enough to establish this himself.

His daughter, the Queen, has been Head of the Commonwealth now for thirty-four years, and the role has developed with her. By her efforts and enthusiasm for the association she has, so to speak, written her own job-description, but what will happen in the future is unclear. The Prince of Wales has shown himself to be a loyal friend of the Commonwealth, but he will not automatically assume the role of Head when he ascends the throne. It has been suggested that this symbolic role might be rotated around the older Commonwealth statesmen, and it is even believed that Idi Amin once offered himself for the job. However, there are a number of worthier figures who would fill the role with impartiality and distinction.

The members of the Commonwealth speak in glowing terms of its usefulness. The Prime Minister of New Zealand, for examples, talks of the many 'high profile' projects in which the Commonwealth is involved today.

> We have Commonwealth student exchange programmes, educational programmes. There are Commonwealth accords or understandings on legal matters, and Commonwealth finance ministers . . . meet to discuss agreed positions at larger international forums. These are the little things which sometimes mean far more than grand resolutions about world affairs. It's actually when you're taking these small steps in mutual co-operation, that you're really making progress.

The Prime Minister of Singapore, Lee Kuan Yew, puts it this way:

> This is a world with many different issues and many different points of view clamouring to be heard. If you are powerful then your lone voice can be heard like that of Mr Reagan or Mr Gorbachev. If you are less powerful and you combine together and form a chorus of harmony, then you stand a better chance of being heard. That's what we do in the Commonwealth.

Papua New Guinea chose to join the Commonwealth because it saw the organisation as a valuable aid to a small country trying to deal with the larger world of international politics. As former Prime Minister Michael Somare says:

> The point about it is, Commonwealth countries

do help one another. We get technical assistance from Commonwealth countries, we are able to exchange views, we can help each other establish things like development corporations and so on.

In my country for example, through one Commonwealth technical co-operation scheme, we were able to get consultants to help us re-negotiate our mineral contracts. Technocrats were actually provided by the Commonwealth Secretariat to help us. That's what the Commonwealth does. It brings people together. It helps the smaller countries unable to make their own way in some sections of international life.

Her Majesty sees that kind of Commonwealth co-operation as the essence of the Commonwealth spirit. In 1968 she said in a Christmas broadcast:

Every individual and every nation has problems, so there is all the more reason for us to do our utmost to show our concern for others.

Rich and poor, we all depend upon the work and skill of individual men and women, particularly those in industry and production who are the creators of wealth and prosperity. Everything we do now is helping shape the world in which our children are going to live.

But with the proliferation of international organisations and groupings such as the UN, NATO, SEATO, the EEC and the OAU, what chance does the voice of the Commonwealth have of being heard on the world stage. Does it have a future at all?

Brian Mulroney, Prime Minister of Canada, gives it a qualified thumbs-up.

If it became silly and vexatious and indulged in meaningless rhetoric and we forgot our roots and our traditions, if we forgot our sense of tolerance and fair-mindedness and our sense of reasonableness . . . then we would become irrelevant – because who would want to listen to a bunch of

Wherever the Queen goes, she always makes a point of addressing young people, for she believes they are the future of the Commonwealth

people sitting around purporting to speak on
behalf of people who care not to be represented
by people like that? And so I suppose we are an
endangered species, potentially, but not if we
keep our sense of history and our sense of
humour and our sense of perspective about
ourselves and the countries we represent and our
responsibilities. If we do that, I think we'll be all
right.

The last word should go to Her Majesty the Queen.
Three years ago she quoted the poet John Donne in a
reference to the continuing need for co-operation within
the Commonwealth. She ended that broadcast with
these words:

The poet John Donne said,'No man is an island,
entire of itself; every man is a piece of the
continent, a part of the main.' That is the message of the Commonwealth.

APPENDIX A

The Queen's Commonwealth Tours

1953-4   The Queen and the Duke of Edinburgh visited Bermuda, Jamaica, Fiji, Tonga, New Zealand, Australia, Ceylon, Uganda, Malta and Gibraltar.

1956   Three-week visit to Nigeria, beginning mid-January.

1957   Visit to Canada, where on 14 October the Queen opened the twenty-third Canadian Parliament, the first Sovereign to open the Canadian Parliament in person.

1959   Six-week tour of Canada in June and July, during which the Queen opened the new St Lawrence Seaway and visited outlying districts in Canada never before seen by a reigning monarch.

1961   Visit to Cyprus, India and Pakistan in the early part of the year, and in November visits to Ghana, Sierra Leone and the Gambia.

1963   In February and March full Royal tours of New Zealand and Australia, visiting Fiji *en route*.

1964   Visit to Canada for the centennial celebrations in October commemorating the visits of the Fathers of Confederation to Charlottetown and Quebec City.

1966   Caribbean tour in February and March.

1967   State visit to Canada for the 100th anniversary of the Confederation and for Expo 67. Also that year in November, the first state visit as Sovereign to an independent Malta.

1970   Tour of Australia and New Zealand, visiting Fiji and Tonga *en route*, from March to May, with Princess Anne and accompanied part of the time by the Prince of Wales. In July the Queen visited Canada to mark the centenaries of the North-West Territories and the province of Manitoba with the Prince of Wales and Princess Anne.

1971   Visit to Canada in May with Princess Anne to attend the Centennial celebrations of the province of British Columbia.

1972   Tour in February and March, accompanied by Princess Anne for part of the time, to Singapore, Malaysia, Brunei, the Maldive Islands, the Seychelles, Mauritius and Kenya.

1973   Visits to Canada and to Australia. In Canada Her Majesty went to Ontario, Prince Edward Island, Saskatchewan and Alberta, and then went to Ottawa for the meeting of the Commonwealth heads of government. In Australia in October the Queen opened the Sydney Opera House.

1974   In January and February, the Queen and the Duke of Edinburgh visited the Cook Islands *en route* to New Zealand. During the New Zealand tour the Queen and the Duke attended the Commonwealth Games. The Queen went on to Norfolk Island, the New Hebrides, the British Solomon Islands and Papua New Guinea. That was followed by a tour of Australia, where Her Majesty opened Parliament. (The Queen returned to London for the general election of that year, while the Duke of Edinburgh continued the tour into March.)

1975   In February, the Queen went to the Commonwealth countries of Barbados and the Bahamas and also visited Bermuda. Later that year, in April, the Queen was in Jamaica for the Commonwealth heads of government meeting. On a visit to the Far East in May, the Queen visited Hong Kong.

1976   Tour of the Canadian provinces of Nova Scotia and New Brunswick before opening and attending the Olympic Games in Montreal. The Queen was accompanied by Prince Andrew and, briefly, by the Prince of Wales and Prince Edward.

1977   Silver Jubilee Year. Tours of Western Samoa, Fiji, Tonga, Papua New Guinea, Australia and New Zealand. Later that year, tours of Canada (Ottawa area only), the Bahamas, Antigua, the British Virgin Islands and Barbados.

1978   Visit to Canada, including Newfoundland, Saskatchewan and Alberta in July and August, during which the Queen attended the Commonwealth Games.

1979   State visits in July and August to Tanzania, Malawi, Botswana and Zambia.

1980   Visit to Australia – Canberra, Sydney and Melbourne – in May.

1981   September and October: visit to Melbourne, Australia, for the Commonwealth heads of government meeting. Also tours of Sydney, Hobart, Perth and Adelaide, before going on to Christchurch, Wellington and Auckland in New Zealand. In mid-October, the Queen undertook a state visit to Sri Lanka.

1982   In April the Queen went to Canada for the Patriation Ceremony in Ottawa. In October she went to Australia, attending the Commonwealth Games in Brisbane, and from there went on a tour of Papua New Guinea, the Solomon Islands, Nauru, Kiribati, Tuvalu and Fiji.

1983   In February and March the Queen visited Jamaica, the Cayman Islands, and British Columbia in Canada. In November Her Majesty made state visits to Kenya, Bangladesh and India and was in New Delhi at the time of the Commonwealth heads of government meeting. The Queen also went to Hyderabad and Poona.

1984   The Queen visited Canada from 24 September to 7 October.

1985   Caribbean tour. The Queen made her first visit to Belize, and then went to the Bahamas to be in Nassau during the Commonwealth heads of government meeting. The rest of her tour included visits to St Kitts Nevis, Antigua, St Lucia, Dominica, St Vincent, the Grenadines, Barbados, Grenada and Trinidad and Tobago.

1986   In February and March the Queen visited New Zealand and Australia.

APPENDIX B

The Declaration of Commonwealth Principles

When Commonwealth heads of government met in Singapore in January 1971 they agreed on a set of ideals which are subscribed to by all members and provide a basis for peace, understanding and goodwill among all mankind. They are expressed in the Declaration of Commonwealth Principles:

The Commonwealth of Nations is a voluntary association of independent sovereign states, each responsible for its own policies, consulting and co-operating in the common interests of their peoples and in the promotion of international understanding and world peace.

Members of the Commonwealth come from territories in the six continents and five oceans, include peoples of different races, languages and religions, and display every stage of economic development from poor developing nations to wealthy industrialised nations. They encompass a rich variety of cultures, traditions and institutions.

Membership of the Commonwealth is compatible with the freedom of member governments to be non-aligned or to belong to any other grouping, association or alliance. Within this diversity all members of the Commonwealth hold certain principles in common. It is by pursuing these principles that the Commonwealth can continue to influence international society for the benefit of mankind.

We believe that international peace and order are essential to the security and prosperity of mankind; we therefore support the United Nations and seek to strengthen its influence for peace in the world, and its efforts to remove the causes of tension between nations.

We believe in the liberty of the individual, in equal rights for all citizens regardless of race, colour, creed or political belief, and in their inalienable right to participate by means of free and democratic political processes in framing the society in which they live. We therefore strive to promote in each of our countries those representative institutions and guarantees for personal freedom under the law that are our common heritage.

We recognise racial prejudice as a dangerous sickness threatening the healthy development of the human race and racial discrimination as an unmitigated evil of society. Each of us will vigorously combat this evil within our own nation. No country will afford to regimes which practise racial discrimination assistance which in its own judgement directly contributes to the pursuit or consolidation of this evil policy.

We oppose all forms of colonial domination and racial oppression and are committed to the principles of human dignity and equality. We will therefore use all our efforts to foster human equality and dignity everywhere, and to further the principles of self-determination and non-racialism.

We believe that the wide disparities in wealth now existing between different sections of mankind are too great to be tolerated. They also create world tensions. Our aim is their progressive removal. We therefore seek to use our efforts to overcome poverty, ignorance and disease, in raising standards of life and achieving a more equitable international society.

To this end our aim is to achieve the freest possible flow of international trade on terms fair and equitable to all, taking into account the special requirements of the developing countries, and to encourage the flow of adequate resources, including governmental and private resources, to the developing countries, bearing in mind the importance of doing this in a true spirit of partnership and of establishing for this purpose in the developing countries conditions which are conducive to sustained investment and growth.

We believe that international co-operation is essential to remove the causes of war, promote tolerance, combat injustice, and secure development among the peoples of the world. We are convinced that the Commonwealth is one of the most fruitful associations for these purposes.

In pursuing these principles the members of the Commonwealth believe that they can provide a constructive example of the multi-national approach which is vital to peace and progress in the modern world. The association is based on consultation, discussion and co-operation.

In rejecting coercion as an instrument of policy they recognise that the security of each member state from external aggression is a matter of concern to all members. It provides many channels for continuing exchanges of knowledge and views on professional, cultural, economic, legal and political issues among member states.

These relationships we intend to foster and extend, for we believe that our multi-national association can expand human understanding and understanding among nations, assist in the elimination of discrimination based on differences of race, colour or creed, maintain and strengthen personal liberty, contribute to the enrichment of life for all, and provide a powerful influence for peace among nations.

INDEX

Aden 33, 133
Alexandra, Princess 109
Amin, Idi 159–60, 176
Andrew, Prince 92, 107, 117, 138, 148, 170
Anne, Princess 20, 27, 35, *36*, 39, 54, 56, 59, 64, 69, *80*, 111, *112*, 138, 169
Antigua and Barbuda xiv, *12*, 14, 120, 122, *124*, 163, 166
Anyaoku, Chief Emeka 154–6
Attlee, Clement 5, 41
Australia xv, 2, 10, *13*, 14, 15, 21, 30–3, 38, 62–9, 77, 80, 81, 92, 95, 101, 136, 138, 144, 148, *151*, 152, 161, 170

Bahamas xiv, *13*, 14, 100, 119, 120, 122, 125–7, *128*, 129, 130–3
Balfour, Lord 3
Banda, Dr Hastings 8, 84, 94, *96*, 159
Bangladesh xv, 11, *13*, 52, 172
Bannister, Roger 139, 140
Barbados xiv, *12*, 14, 118, 119–20, 122, 123
Belize (Brit. Honduras) xiv, *13*, 14, 122, 123–5
Bermuda 21, 138
Bhutto, Zulfikar Ali 161
Biko, Steve 161–2
Bishop, Maurice 123
Bolkiah, Sultan Hassanal 59–60
Botswana (Bechuanaland) xiv, *13*, 84, 92, *93*, 94
Britannia, HMS *18*, 22, 35–8, 59, 60, 68, 100, 105, 107, 109, *113*, 126, 127–9, 131–4
Brunei xv, 11, *12*, 15, 59–60
Burma 2

Callaghan, James 153, 159
Canada xiv, 2, 10, *12*, 14, 57, 101–17, 136, 139, 148, 161, 164, 170
Ceylon *see* Sri Lanka
Chamberlain, Neville 91
Charles, Eugenia xvi, 17, 165
Charles, Prince of Wales 20, 27, 35, *36*, 39, 64, 65, 69, 75, 77, 86, 111, *112*, *116*, 122, 138, 141, 146, 169–70, 175–6
Christmas broadcasts *xvii*, 21, 27, 28, 38, 41, 49, 52, 56, 129–30, 172, 173, 177, 180
Churchill, Winston 5, 37, 41, 119
Commonwealth Games 135–52
Commonwealth heads of government meetings 6–8, *9*, 11, *15*, *18*, 56, 64, 94–9, 100, 111, 120, 125, 159, 160, 163–6
Commonwealth Principles 186–7
Cook, Captain 70, 79
Cook Island 77, *80*
Curzon, Lord 40, 57

Cyprus xiv, 9–10, *13*, 159

De Gaulle, General Charles 105
Diana, Princess of Wales 69, 75
Diefenbaker, John 107, 114
Dominica xiv, *13*, 17, 103, 120, 122, 123, 165

East Africa 21, 84
Edinburgh, Duke of 17, *18*, 20, 21, *23–7*, 29, *31–5*, 37, 38, 39, 42,
    44–6, 54, 59, *60*, *63*, *64*, *66*, 70, 71, 75, 78, 79, *81*, *83*, *86*, *87*, *89*,
    92, 101, *104*, 105, *106*, 107, *108*, 109, *110*, *112*, 131, 138, 140, *142*,
    145, 146, 148–9, 157, 161, 169, 170
Edward, Prince 138, 148, 170
Eisenhower, Dwight 107
Elizabeth, the Queen Mother 38, 39, 109, 157, 170
Elizabeth II, Queen (photographs) *xvii*, *9*, *15*, *18*, *23–7*, *30–6*, *42–5*,
    28, *50–3*, *55*, *58*, *60*, *61*, *63*, *65*, *66*, *71–4*, *77–81*, *83–7*, *89*, *93*,
    96, *97*, *102*, *104*, *106*, *108*, *110*, *112*, *116*, *119*, *121*, *124*, *150*,
    158, *167*, *171*, *178*, *179*
  as Commonwealth leader xvi–xvii, 14, 15–19, 20, 21, 28–9, 38–9,
    41, 49, 58–9, 61, 68, 76, 85–6, 90–3, 95, 98–100, 102, 105, 111,
    122, 125, 129–30, 138, 152, 153, 157–9, 162, 165–6, 170–2, 173,
    175–6, 177, 180
  and Commonwealth tours
    of Africa 20–1, 23, 33–5, 83–100
    of Australia 21, 31–3, 62–9
    of Canada 101–17
    of Caribbean 21–2, 118–34
    of India, Sri Lanka (Ceylon), Pakistan and Bangladesh 33–4,
      40–57
    of New Zealand 21, 26–31, 69–77
    of Pacific islands 22–3, 24–6, 36, 77–81, 161
    of South-East Asia 57–61
  and Royal Family 20–1, 27, 39, 64, 69, 107–9, 112, 118, 138, 148,
    170
Elliot, Herb 139, *142*

Falkland Islands 149
Fiji xv, *13*, 14, 22–4, 38, 77, 109, 135, 138, 161, 165, 166
Fraser, Malcolm 64, 82, 159

Gambia, the xiv, 2, *12*, 82, 109
Gandhi, Indira 54, *55*, 56, 165
Gandhi, Mahatma 41, *44*, 54
Gandhi, Rajiv xvii, 16, 56–7, 114
George V, King *4*, 40, 44, 54, 136, 137
George VI, King 20, 21, 41, 91, 175
Gloucester, Duke of 157
Ghana (Gold Coast) xiv, 2, 8, *12*, 82, 86–92, 115, 135
Gibraltar 37
Gilbert and Ellice Islands 77
Gorton, John 68–9
Gothic, SS 22, 24, 26, 33, 109
Grenada xiv, *12*, 14, 15, 120, 122

Guyana xiv, *13*, 120, 154

Hawke, Robert xvi, 66–7, 68
Heath, Edward 100
Hitler, Adolf 91
Home, Alec Douglas 173
Hong Kong *61*, 138

India xiii, xv, 2, 5–8, 11, *13*, 38, 40–57, 114, 115, 138, 172, 175
Irish Republic 10–11

Jamaica xiv, *13*, 14, *22*, 38, 120, 135, 138, 146, 164, 166

Kaunda, Kenneth xvi, 8, 56, 84, 92, *96*, 98, 99, 159
Keino, Kip 135, 146, *147*
Kenya xiv, 9, *12*, 21, 52, 84, *97*, 135
Kenyatta, Jomo 9, *97*
Kerr, Sir John 15, 64, 65
Kiribati xv, *12*, 77, 78

Lange, David xvii, 16, 75, 76, 98, 176
Lee Kuan Yew 1, 58–9, 165, 176
Lesotho (Basutoland) xiv, *12*, 15, 84, 159

Makarios, Archbishop 10, 159
Malawi (Nyasaland) xiv, 8, *13*, 84, 92, 159
Malaya 2, 9, 57
Malaysia xv, *13*, 15, 57–60
Maldives, the xv, *13*, 60–1
Malta xiv, *12*, *36*, 37
Maoris 70, *74*, 75
Margaret, Princess 38, 39, 71, 118
Marshall, Sir Peter 156
Mary, Queen 153–4, 156
Mauritius xv, *12*, 14, *60*, 61, 103
Middle East 2–3
Mohamed, Dr Mahathir xvi, 16, 59
Montagu, Edwin 40–1
Moshoeshoe, King 159
Mountbatten, Lord Louis 5, 6, 37
Mugabe, Robert 56
Mulroney, Brian xvi, 16, 57, 101, 103, 114, 177–8
Muzorewa, Bishop Abel 92, 93

Nauru xv, *12*, 61, 77, 78
Nehru, Jawaharlal 5, 6–7, 8, *43*
New Zealand xv, 2, *13*, 14, 21, 26–31, 38, 63, 64, 69–77, 101, 136, 138, 148, *150*, 161
Nigeria xiv, *13*, 82, *83*, *84*, *86*, 95, 135, 138
Nkomo, Joshua 92, 93
Nkrumah, Kwame 8, *9*, 87, 89–90
Nyerere, Julius 1, 84, 156, 165

Obote, Milton 56
Ogilvy, Hon. Angus 109
Owen, Dr David 94, 160

Pakistan 6, 8, 11, 38, 40, 41, 46–7, 52, 57, 115, 161
Papua New Guinea xiii, xv, *13*, 14, 39, 62, 77, 80–1, 161, 176–7

Rahman, Tunku Abdul 57, 58
Ramphal, Sir Shridath 'Sonny' 57, 98, 154, *155*
Rhodesia 90–4, 95, 98, 100, 114, 138; *see also* Zimbabwe

Sabah (N. Borneo) 58, 59
St Christopher Nevis xiv, *12*, 14, 120, *121*, 122
St Lucia xiv, *12*, 14, 103, 122, 166
St Vincent and the Grenadines xiv, *12*, 14, 120, 122, 135
Salote, Queen of Tonga *25*, 26, 78
Sarawak 58, 59
Scoon, Sir Paul 15, 123
Seychelles xv, 10, *13*, 61
Shrivastava, K. P. 162–3
Sierra Leone xiv, 13, 82, *85*
Singapore xv, *13*, 57, 58, 60, 138
Singh, President of India 56
Smith, Arnold 91, 157, 165, 174–5
Smith, Ian 90–1
Sobers, Sir Garfield 122, *124*
Solomon Islands xv, *12*, 14, 77
Somare, Michael 62, 80–1, 176–7
South Africa 2, 10, 11, 20, 21, 23, 57, 100, 101, 114, 136, 138,
    142–4, 161
Sri Lanka (Ceylon) xv, 2, 8, *12*, 33, *34*, *35*, 38, 57, 138
Swaziland xiv, *12*, 15, 84

Tanzania (Tanganyika and Zanzibar) xiv, *13*, 84, 92, 94, 98, 156, 168
Taufa'ahau Tupou IV, King 78, *79*
Teresa of Calcutta, Mother *53*
Thatcher, Margaret xvii, 38, 56, 57, 92, 95, 100, 114, 123
Tonga xv, *13*, 15, 22, 24–6, 38, 78, 109, 161
Trinidad and Tobago xiv, *13*, 120, 122, 135, 138
Trudeau, Pierre 102, 111–12, 127, 165
Tuvalu xv, 11, *12*, 14, 61, 77, *78*, 78, 135

Uganda xiv, *12*, 33, 38, 84, 159, 161
United States of America 7–8, 10, 101, 115, 122, 123, 126

Vanuatu xiv, 11, *12*, 78, 103
Victoria, Queen 3, 70

West Africa 2, 82
Western Samoa xv, *13*, 78, *79*, 161
West Indies 2, 118–34, 161, 166
Whitlam, Gough 15, 64, 65, 165
William, Prince 69
Wilson, Harold 90, 91, 114, 159, 165

Zambia (Northern Rhodesia) xiii, xiv, 8, *13*, 84, 92–4, 95, *96*, 98,
    99, 159
Zimbabwe (Southern Rhodesia) xiv, 9, *13*, 84